INVESTING

FOR BEGINNERS

Simple Investing Guide to Become an Intelligent Investor and Grow Your Wealth Continuously

Preface

Who is This Book For?

Before we dive right in, I need to make sure that you are the right audience for this book. If you have done extensive Google searches for investment strategies or you've actually tried your hand at stock investment, bond selection or mutual fund analysis, this book is not for you. If you are a seasoned investor who is looking for a strategic edge on how to maximize your return on investment, again, this book is not for you. Even if you are a complete newbie investor who hasn't yet invested in the stock market, but knows a few concepts, this book is not for you.

This book is for absolute beginners. I can't emphasize this enough. If you have only managed to save a few dollars in your bank account, but have no idea what to do next, this book is for you.

This book is for absolute beginners. These are people who have some money saved up, but have absolutely no understanding of investing.

You may have thought about growing your money. You may have thought about what to do next after saving a few bucks in the bank. As long as you haven't done any investigation as to how to grow your accumulated capital, this book is for you.

Keep in mind that this book doesn't teach you how to save. It already assumes that you have money saved up. It also assumes that you are just looking for broad ideas on how to grow whatever you've saved.

If you're looking for deeply intricate and highly complicated investment strategies and processes, this book is not for you. Instead, this book paints in broad strokes what you can do to grow your money.

I don't go into heavy duty detail, I just want to open your mind as to the broad array of investment possibilities you have available to you. Once you have gotten a general understanding of the investment possibilities, the next step is to drill down, to look at specific investment vehicles, particular investment strategies, as well as the advantages and disadvantages they bring to the table.

My purpose is writing this book is to open your mind to the broad array of possibilities available to you if you are serious about growing your money. Keep in mind that investments don't just involve stocks and bonds. Investments don't just involve your 401K or your IRA. There are actually so many other investment opportunities and pathways for growing your wealth available out there.

Table of Contents

Introduction...7

Chapter 1: Understand Why You Need to Grow Your Money 9

Chapter 2: Understand How Compound Growth Works When You Invest Your Money...15

Chapter 3: How Investments Work in General....................19

Chapter 4: Before You Invest, Know Yourself.....................24

Chapter 5: Don't Let the Government Eat Up Your Investment 28

Chapter 6: Quick Introduction to Asset Classes..................32

Chapter 7: Stock Investing: The What, Where, When, How, and Why...39

Chapter 8: Investing in Real Estate 55

Chapter 9: Investing in Bonds 66

Chapter 10: Investing in Business Partnerships..................72

Chapter 11: Investing in Private Corporations....................79

Chapter 12: Investing in Precious Metals..........................84

Chapter 13: Investment Vehicles 92

Chapter 14: Getting Organized: How to Form Your Own Personal Investing Plan 97

Chapter 15: Investment Strategies 101

Conclusion 109

Introduction

If you're reading this book, you have some cash saved in the bank and you're thinking of growing your money. If this is the case, then you're definitely on the right track.

You are definitely on the right track because most people don't get to that stage. In fact, according to a recent survey, most Americans are living paycheck to paycheck. In fact, if they were forced to write a check for $2,000, half of America's households cannot cut that check. That's how bad things are when it comes to savings.

So if you have some cash saved in the bank and you are looking for ways to grow that pile of money, you are definitely on the right track. You are a responsible person, you are a forward thinker, and you have the raw ingredients to make that money work for you instead of you constantly having to work for your money.

The Bad News

Now for the bad news. Regardless of how much cash you may have saved, you need to grow your money because it is losing value every single day it sits in the bank. I know this is hard to believe because the $5,000 you have in your account still says $5,000 after several months sitting in the bank. When you check your statement, it says pretty much the same amount of money.

In fact, thanks to the interest being paid to you by the bank, it seems that your money is even growing by a small fraction. Well, don't get too excited. Every year, your money is able to buy less and less goods and services. This is called inflation.

Whatever your saved dollars can buy this year, will buy less next year. And it gets worse after that. In fact, the amount of products and services your money can buy on a year to year basis continues to go down. Unless you do something, your money won't be able to buy much of anything at a particular point in the future.

If you find this all hard to believe, keep in mind that in the 1930's, you could buy a house for $1,000. You could buy a car for a couple of hundred dollars. In fact, meals can be had for pennies. That's how much the US dollar has sunk in value over the decades.

Inflation is very much real and if you are not careful, the money that you worked so hard for to save up in the bank won't be able to do you much good, thanks to inflation. The worst part to all of this is that your money might deteriorate in value to such an extent that you would be putting yourself in a really tight spot at the point in your life where you are most vulnerable. I am of course talking about your retirement.

Do yourself a big favor and prepare for a better retirement future by deciding to simply get the most value out of the hard earned dollars you have stored away.

This book explores, in broad terms, the different ways you can grow the value of the money that you have saved up. This is money that you worked hard for. This is money that you sacrificed and sweated for. Make sure that it retains its value.

In fact, you should make sure that it grows in value over time instead of being eaten up by inflation. This book will not only open your mind to the prospect of increasing the value of your money, but hopefully get you excited about the whole investment process.

Chapter 1: Understand Why You Need to Grow Your Money

In the introduction, I gave you a quick summary of why you need to grow your money. In this chapter, we're going to dive in a little bit deeper into inflation and reduction in purchasing power.

The reason why I need to drive this point home is that it's very easy to treat inflation as some sort of intellectual construct. It's easy to think of it as some sort of idea that affects other people, but passes you by. Believe me, inflation hits everybody.

In fact, inflation is so efficient that it works almost like clockwork. Unless you invested the right way, inflation will hit you. Even if you make good money now at your job, inflation will make sure that your hard earned dollars won't stretch as much as they used to. Inflation is that bad.

Saving is Great and is Crucial, But It isn't Enough

You probably are thinking that you've won most of the battle when it comes to personal financial management the moment you've learned to save. I can't say I blame you for thinking along these lines because most people can't even get around to saving. They're always looking at their expenses. They're always looking at their long term liabilities and they never really get around to saving much of anything.

If anything, savings happens at the end of the budget process. They would get their income, and then they would immediately take out their expenses and their liabilities and whatever is left over maybe goes to savings, assuming it survives luxury expenses or entertainment expenses. It is no surprise that given this situation, most Americans don't even have $2,000 in the bank.

As I've mentioned in the introduction, if they were forced by circumstances to cut a check for $2,000, almost half of American households cannot cut that check. They know it's going to bounce. They know they're going to get into trouble if they issue that check. That's how bad things are on a household to household basis, as far as American personal financial management goes.

Since you are able to save, you have overcome that. You have developed a very powerful discipline that enables you to pay yourself first. A lot of people budget their income in a way where savings comes last. You and other savers, on the other hand, think differently. You pay yourself first.

What you do is you take your income and you set aside savings first and everything else that's left will be divvied up among expenses and liabilities. This is absolutely the correct way to do things. It's rough at first, it takes some getting used to, but the more you do it, the better you get at it. And I definitely congratulate you for having developed the discipline and personal financial skill to be able to pull this off.

However, as awesome as this accomplishment may be, it isn't enough. Saving is crucial for effective personal financial management, but simply saving or putting money in the bank is a losing game. Why? The 800 pound gorilla called inflation.

The Very Real Threat of Inflation

Before we get an understanding of why inflation is so bad, it's a good idea to talk about where inflation comes from. Why is it that the price of goods and services tend to rise over time?

Let's put it this way, if you walked into a Taco Bell 12 years ago, I can guarantee you that the prices on the menu look way different than their current price list. This is guaranteed. Why? Food prices, just like with everything else, tend to go up over time.

Sure, there are certain categorical exemptions, but for the most part, this is true. In fact, this applies to almost all product categories. Whether we're looking at clothing, computer items, stereo equipment, and so on and so forth, the prices of goods tend to go up over time.

However, thanks to the outsourcing of manufacturing to China, a lot of the inflationary pressure on consumer goods have dropped fairly recently. It's anybody's guess how long this will continue. We seem to have gotten quite a bit of a break, thanks to the miracles of modern globalized mass manufacturing, which enables Walmart to sell products cheaper and cheaper by the year. That is the exception that proves the rule.

For everything else, especially services, prices tend to go up over time. The reason for this is due to money supply. You have to understand that unlike the olden days, the value of money is no longer tied to a physical object.

For the longest time, the value of the US dollar, as well as other currencies, was tied to gold or, to a lesser degree, silver. There was some sort of physical frame of reference for the value of money. While governments did play fast and loose with how they arrived at the value of their money or how they fixed the value of their money, for the most part, they still had a frame of reference that is tied to a precious metal.

Since there is that link to real world industrial value as represented by that precious metal, governments can't go crazy with valuation. They can't just print out money with abandon and expect the market to take care of it. It doesn't work that way. They are forced to establish some sort of discipline because their money is at least superficially backed up by gold or some sort of precious metal.

Well, nowadays, money only has value because the issuing government behind that money says that it has value. In other words, the global economy works on a "trust me" basis. This is why when global financial traders lose confidence in a government, that government's currency crashes. Look at the case of Zimbabwe for the most recent case study of this effect.

When Zimbabwe, starting in the early 2000's, started nationalizing white-farmer owned farms, it collapsed the economy. At a certain point, the Zimbabwe government was printing out notes in trillion denominations and it still wasn't enough to buy you a dozen eggs or a loaf of bread. If this sounds familiar, it is because this happens in almost all decades to many different economies.

For example, in the 1920's, this happened in Germany. People would take a wheelbarrow, fill it up with paper cash to buy a loaf of bread. This is the real problem with money that has no confidence. And unfortunately, when governments constantly print out billions upon billions of paper notes every single year, this has the residual effect of depressing purchasing value.

This is the real reason for inflation. It's all about money supply, as well as relative confidence in the currency, and the economy behind that currency. As you can probably already tell, there is a very real threat of inflation because it's always going up.

You have to find a way to protect the value of your money. Otherwise, regardless of how much cash you have saved up today, it's not going to buy much in the future because prices have shot through the roof.

Investing Grows Your Money

Investing grows the value of the money that you've saved up in the bank. That is the long and short of investing. The reason you're investing is because you want to end up with more than what you started. You also want to end up with more than what the bank will pay you in the form of interest.

You have to understand that keeping your money in the bank to collect interest is a losing game. Why? Not only is the interest pitifully low and always below the rate of inflation, you also get taxed on the appreciation of your money. In other words, you lose twice. That's why it's really important to make sure that you only put money in the bank as a temporary strategy while you're figuring where to ultimately invest your money.

Focus on investing your money instead of keeping it in cash form. Keeping your money in cash partially is always a good idea because you don't know what the future will bring. However, it is also always a bad idea to keep all your money in the form of cash because of inflation.

Investing enables you to grow your money. That is the core of investing. With that said, there are different ways to grow your money.

Asset Classes

Asset classes are a fancy economic term for the different kinds of ways you can grow your money. You buy assets that differ from each other and these assets, categorically speaking, have different rates of appreciation. In other words, they grow your money at different rates.

It's important to note that when people talk about "investing," they almost always talk about stocks and bonds. But these two types of assets, as big and popular as they may be, are just two of many. You can try real estate, you can try passive income businesses, you can try active businesses, you can try precious metals. There are many different ways you can grow money, and this book will step you through some of the more common investment asset classes you can get into.

Chapter 2: Understand How Compound Growth Works When You Invest Your Money

Anybody who is looking to transition from being a saver to an investor must first cut their teeth on the importance of compound growth. Compound growth works when you keep putting in money in your investments and they keep growing over time.

In other words, instead of just investing once in the past and forgetting about it, you continue to invest in consistent and constant increments so that your base of assets keeps growing and growing. Your older base appreciates to a certain degree, but this is followed up by a lesser appreciation for your more current investments.

If you were to add all of those investments up, they add to a lot more money than if you decided to invest a big amount last week. Why? Since your money has been sitting in the stock market or in the real estate market for a long enough period of time, it has appreciated considerably.

So if you were to constantly put money in investments, the value of your money increases tremendously because you're making new investments, while older investments increase in value. In other words, you're simply building on the value base that you have built up from before.

This is why compounding is such a powerful force in personal finance. In fact, one of its biggest fans is Albert Einstein. With his massive intellect, he clearly saw the power of compounding.

The great thing about compounding is that it may start small, but as long as you're constantly adding to your investment, it continues to increase, especially if you do this over a fairly long period of time.

Different Ways of Measuring Investment Returns

Without boring you or scaring you with technical terms, I need to discuss with you the concept of "returns." When you first start investing, you probably are thinking that you just want to get more money than you put in. This is pretty basic.

If you are thinking along these lines, you are definitely on the right path. You know you are doing something wrong when you put in money in an investment and out comes less money than you put in. Most people can tell whether they're losing money or they're gaining money.

Now that you are clear that you want to gain money, the next step is to learn how to measure those gains the right way. Keep in mind that when you receive more money than you put in, this is called a return. This is a good thing. But this, of course, is not enough.

You have to be clear as to how to compare or judge the return that you get from one type of investment compared to another type of investment or another investment opportunity. This is where concepts like alpha and beta come in. While I'm not going to obsess too much about these specific benchmarks, it's important to note what they represent.

An alpha return metric is usually used in the stock market. The alpha measures the return on investment that you get for a particular stock compared to the index. Meaning, if you were to average out, with some adjustments, all the leading stocks of a certain collection of industries, you would get an average performance for the market as a whole. Your investment's alpha measurement clearly tells you whether the returns that you're getting from a particular stock are above average, average or below average.

While you may not be interested in investing in stocks, you should still think along the same lines. For example, if you are thinking of investing in precious metals or real estate, look at the return of investment that you're getting from those asset classes and compare them to the average within those asset classes.

For example, if you are investing in real estate and you've got into an REIT, look at the return of investment that you got from that particular investment compared to REITs, generally speaking, or better yet, the return on investment on the specific real estate market your REIT is invested in. This should give you a clearer picture of whether you are getting a good return or a mediocre one.

Keep in mind that just because you're getting more money than you put in, this is not enough. You have to compare it to something else.

Similarly, the beta metric measures how volatile your particular investment is compared to the market your investment is part of. For example, if you bought a stock, you notice the ups and downs of that stock over a certain period of time. Now compare how much it swings to the rest of the market. This is a good measurement not of return, but of risk. In other words, how likely is it for your investment to go from nasty to really heady upswings and nasty down swings.

This is a very important detail to keep in mind because not everybody can handle the stress of up and down market movements equally. Some people are risk averse. They don't like risks. They're not big on surprises. Other people understand that the greater the risks, the greater the rewards. So they're more tolerant of up and down swings.

Still, regardless of what asset class you're thinking of investing in, pay attention to beta or measurements of volatility because this can also guide you in buying certain investments within the same asset class that you feel are less volatile than others.

These two metrics work hand in hand. Alpha and beta must always be in your mind, not necessarily in technical terms, but instead, focus more on the ideas that they represent. Again, the return must be in the context of how the rest of the market in that asset class performs. Risk profile or volatility must also be measured by the general risk profile of the other assets in that asset class.

Chapter 3: How Investments Work in General

If you're trying to grow your money, you have actually many methods at your disposal. There are many ways to grow your money and end up with more cash than when you started. Investments are just one of them. You can loan out your money, you can put your money in savings accounts or similar instruments like certificate of deposits and treasury notes.

The Difference Between Investments and Loans

When you loan out your money, the person or company that takes out the loan (the borrower) is under legal obligation to not only give you your money back, but also provide a return for the money you loaned that person. This is called "interest." The amount you let that person borrow is called the "principal."

Your profit in this scenario is, at least in terms of the law, is guaranteed. This person has no choice but to pay it back, unless the person goes bankrupt or there is some other legal reason that would justify that person not paying you back. Still, in terms of getting your money back, loans, at least on a superficial level, guarantee a return. The person has no choice but to pay you back.

Ideally, the best kind of loans involves the government. Basically, you issue a loan to a borrower, but the government steps in and guarantees that if the borrower cannot pay for whatever reason, the government will pay for the loan. This was the idea behind the Fannie Mae housing loan program by the United States government.

Other governments have similar programs. The idea is for the government to enable people with low income to be able to afford homes. The ultimate guarantor of those loans is the federal government.

It's very easy to see why this is such a great deal for private lenders such as yourself. If there is a government program guaranteeing the loan, you don't have to worry whether the person who took out the loan can pay because the government will step in. Since the government has unlimited taxing power, unlike private institutions, you can rest assured that your money will return to you, plus interest.

An investment, on the other hand, doesn't have such guarantees. Whether a borrower is backed up by a third party or not, that person is legally obligated to pay you the principal, plus interest. When you invest that money, however, there is no guarantee that that money will come back. You just take a leap of faith that the investment will turn out well and you will not only get your money back, and a nice return.

Whether you're investing in stocks or mutual funds or real estate and other types of investments, there's always a possibility that you would lose your money. Even if you were to invest in a bond fund, for example, - a mutual fund that specializes in investing in bonds - you can still lose your shirt.

While bonds are technically loans, keep in mind that when you buy a bond from a corporation, that corporation can suffer hard times and be forced to declare bankruptcy. This does happen, and guess what happens to the holders of that company's bonds? While under the law, they get first priority to divide whatever assets are left by the company during bankruptcy, usually, the company has racked up so much debt and obligations that bond holders get only cents on the dollar.

Ultimately, the fact that you invested in bonds, in and of itself, does not give the same guarantees as if you had simply loaned your money to a borrower.

Investment Vs. Savings

When you save money at a bank or you take out a certificate of deposit or invest your money in a term deposit, the bank will guarantee you a published interest rate. This means that you get your money back plus an extra amount called the interest. Sounds good so far, right?

Well, the problem with savings interest-bearing accounts and certificates of deposits, as well as time deposits, is that the interest rate being offered is almost always lower than the rate of inflation. As mentioned earlier, inflation is constantly eating up the value of your money.

If you invest in an interest bearing account, you are usually losing your fight against inflation. To add insult to injury, the government taxes whatever interest income you make off your money. Talk about rubbing it in.

Investments, on the other hand, are so varied and there are so many different options is terms of returns that you can take a calculated risk as to what kind of return you want. For example, historically, stocks have yielded an annual percentage appreciation of over 10%. Good luck finding that kind of return with a savings account or a term deposit account.

While there are very risky banks that would pay out higher interest rates, they only do so because there is a risk that they might go under. That's why they are highly motivated in getting people to deposit their money for long stretches of time. That's why they offer a higher than average interest rates.

The problem is that they also have a higher than average risk of possibly going belly up or otherwise experiencing a crunch that would prevent them from paying out interests. The great advantage of investments is that you tend to get higher returns compared to low risk savings programs.

Investments Vs. Government Instruments

The best investment if you are really scared of risk is, of course, the government. The US government and other governments around the world routinely issue bonds. These are basically IOU notes. They promise, that whoever bears those bonds, a certain return for whatever money they invest.

The great thing about government-backed securities is that the government is not going to go bankrupt any time soon. It can choose to raise taxes, it can choose to collect money in a wide number of ways, so funding, unlike that of a private company, is not an issue.

Now with that said, the drawback to government-backed loans is the possibility of default. While the government may default on their loans, they would still honor them, but the value of the loans would go down.
This is very rare and it usually happens to less stable economies, but it's still a possibility. Maybe the world experiences such a crippling financial crash that the US government is forced to disregard its loans or devalue its loans. It's a very remote possibility, but it can still happen.

On the whole, however, government-backed securities offer much more security to people who are terrified of risk. The downside is that there's so many people buying up government-backed securities that their interest rates or yields are fairly low.

There's really no incentive for the government to pay really high interest rates if it doesn't have to. This is especially true of debt instruments from the Bank of Japan. Japan is one of the most stable economies in the world and a lot of global investors buy up Japanese debt as a safe investment. When there's a tremendous amount of demand, the yields go down. Still, if you're looking for security and assurance that your money will come back, government-backed securities is definitely a good option.

Compare this with investments. When you invest, whether in stocks, bonds or private businesses, you have a chance of getting a much higher return. You may have invested an x amount of money and what will come back is that amount of money plus a nice return. Depending on what you invest in, the return might beat inflation, as well as the interest rate paid out by government debt. The downside to investing, of course, is that you can lose your investment. There is no guarantee that you will get your money back.

Chapter 4: Before You Invest, Know Yourself

Before you even think of investing the money that you have saved up in the bank, you need to do some serious self assessment. You really have to go out of your way to try to understand what your investment profile is. There are two key factors that you need to focus on: risk tolerance and risk profile. You can't confuse these two.

Also, you have to make sure that you are completely honest with yourself regarding these two factors. If you get your signals mixed or you're confused as to these two very important investment factors, it's very easy for you to make the wrong investment decisions. It's very easy for you to invest in asset classes and specific investments that might lead to you losing money.

Just because other people have different risk tolerance and risk profiles, it doesn't necessarily mean that you have to copy them. In fact, if you copy them, you might find out that their particular investment style doesn't fit you. You might have different priorities.

Risk Tolerance

Your age actually has a lot to do with your risk tolerance. Risk tolerance boils down to how much risk you can take on. This may seem pretty straightforward. You are a risk taker, you might be thinking that you would be able to bet all of your savings on a risky stock. That would be a foolish way of assessing risk tolerance. Instead, you should look at your risk tolerance based on one simple metric: How long would it take for you to earn back the amount of money you invested and lost?

In other words, risk tolerance measures your ability to gather the same amount of resources if your investment failed. You have to look at your risk tolerance from this perspective because it has nothing to do with how courageous you are. It has nothing to do with how well you can handle adversity. Instead, it assumes that if you are younger, you have a lot more opportunities to earn your investment capital back.

Whether you work for that capital or you start businesses to recoup that capital, you have to have enough time to earn that money back. This is why age is such a big factor. When you're younger, you simply have more time to recover from investment failures.

On the other side of the spectrum are older people. If you are older and you're getting close to retirement age, you really can't afford to take big risks. You should focus on less risky investments like government-backed securities.

As you get closer to retirement age, you can't earn your investment cash back as quickly as if you were in your 20's. In fact, if you are really close to the age of 65, it's almost all but impossible for you to earn back your life's savings.

Accordingly, your risk tolerance should be on the conservative side. While you may be a very courageous person and you can definitely see the upside of making the right investment at the right time to produce the right returns, in practical terms, you just might not have enough time to recoup your investment should things go south.

Risk Profile

Your risk profile indicates your personal comfort level with particular types of investments. As mentioned in a previous chapter, some investments are less risky than others. For example, government-backed securities are not very risky at all. While there's always a remote chance of a government default, it's so remote that it's not really a consideration. This is why if you're looking for a very conservative investment, you should look into government-backed securities like national bonds, state bonds and even municipal bonds.

Your risk profile measures your personal risk tolerance. In other words, it indicates how courageous you are when it comes to investment choices.

Different asset classes have different risk profiles. For example, real estate has historically been a conservative investment vehicle. However, within real estate, there are riskier deals and less risky deals.

You have to also pay attention to your risk profile when you decide to invest. Different asset classes appeal to different people of different risk profiles. Stocks, on average, have a higher risk profile than bonds. Bonds, on average, have a higher risk profile than government-backed securities. And on and on it goes.

You should look at your risk tolerance and your risk profile. You have to come up with a happy balance between the two factors, otherwise, you might simply be rolling the dice with your hard earned money.

If you are past the age of 50, for example, you have to be really careful about where to invest your nest egg because if things go south, you really don't have that much time to get your money back. You might want to look at the different risk profiles of asset classes available to you to identify a nice middle ground between a nice return and a manageable level of risk.

You have to weigh everything based on your risk tolerance. You have to make an educated guess as to which investments are secure enough so as to protect you from losing your money, but at the same time, have enough risk so that the reward meets your expectations. The general rule when it comes to risk and investments is: The higher the risk, the higher the reward. The more speculative an investment, the higher its return.

Usually, less people bet on that risk investment because it's very, very risky. To attract more investors, the return has to be there. It kind of feeds on itself. The most obvious example of this is junk bonds. Junk bonds tend to pay a higher rate of return precisely because they are so risky. Investors demand a higher rate due to their higher risk.

You have to always weigh your risk profile and your risk tolerance. You don't want to get too far ahead of yourself. You don't want to focus so much on the return that you overlook the fact that to get that return, you have to assume a ridiculous amount of risk.

I hope you can see how this works. You have to know yourself. You have to be completely honest regarding your risk profile and your risk tolerance. If you assume that just because some investors that you admire have a certain risk tolerance and risk profile mix that you simply need to copy them, you might be greatly disappointed. In fact, you might end up worrying a lot because they might have such a higher tolerance of risk than you.

It's perfectly okay to be scared or risk. What's important is that you need to be clear as to what you're working with in terms of personal comfort levels and try to find the best option possible by weighing or cross referencing your risk tolerance with your risk profile so you can identify the right investment asset classes and pick out the right investment options. Blindly following other people's investment advice without cross referencing such advice against your risk tolerance and risk profile is a sure recipe for disaster.

Chapter 5: Don't Let the Government Eat Up Your Investment

Make no mistake about it, when it comes to any kind of income, the government will always be involved. As you probably already know, when it comes to certainty in life, there are really only two things that you can count on: death and taxes. Somehow, some way, they will happen. Get used to it. That's just the way things are.

Taxes are definitely part of the mix when it comes to investment. You probably have heard all sorts of tall tales of certain types of investments that are completely tax free or protect you from all sorts of taxes. You might want to take those tall tales with a grain of salt.

Taxes will always be part of the picture. What's important, however, is to be as clear as possible regarding how taxes are triggered. By knowing which investments incur which taxes, you can plan ahead. You can then weigh your different options.

There are many investments available that produce a fairly high return on investment. However, if their tax rates are also very high, if you factor in your risk as well as the amount of time your money's going to get tied up, those seemingly attractive investments might not turn out to be so attractive after all. I hope you see how this works.

You have to always factor in potential taxes. You will have to pay a tax on the income that you produce from your investment. The only question is how big of a role would this play when it comes to you choosing one investment opportunity over another. Keep in mind the following discussion.

How Investment Taxation Works

Investments are not immune to taxes. Let's just get that out of the way. There are all sorts of investment managers making all sorts of claims regarding "tax proof investments." Don't believe the hype. From a purely technical basis, they don't exist.

At some point in time, the taxes are going to be taken out. You just have to pay attention to the fine print. You might not be conscious of the tax being taken out, but at some point in time, it is being taken out. Even supposedly tax free government investments also have taxes taken out.

Don't fall for the hype. Don't fall for the packaging. Instead, accept the fact that you would have to pay taxes at some point in time.

The issue is how much of a role would the tax play in your overall calculation of the value of the investment opportunity you're considering. That should be the question you wrap your mind around because that spells the difference between what is a solid investment and an investment that may look good on paper, but in reality doesn't really measure up to its alternatives.

Investment taxation has three distinct forms. Again, regardless of what you're going to be investing in, the taxes will be involved. Either you're taxed up front or you're taxed later, taxes are still part of the picture.

Regular or Ordinary Income

If you trade in stocks and you trade regularly, whatever profit you make is subject to ordinary tax. This means that if you make a certain amount of money, the applicable tax bracket would be applied to your profits and you'll be taxed accordingly. Put simply, there's really not much difference between the income you make from active trading from the income you make at a job. In the eyes of the law, it's still ordinary income.

The same applies to rent that you collect from the apartment units that you invested in or commercial property. This is still part of ordinary income. You log the amount of money coming in, you adjust your income based on your expenses and deductions, and then you are taxed based on the profits.

The only exception to regular or ordinary income taxation is if you are engaged in an investment vehicle that is, by law, subject to capital gains tax or qualifies for "deferred" taxation. It's important to keep in mind that the designation of your investment plays a big role in when you get taxed and how much.

A lot of investors get tripped up by capital gains tax. For example, when people try their hand at stock investing, a lot of these newbie investors think that they would be subject to capital gains tax. What they fail to realize is that capital gains tax is very specific. You pay a special tax rate only if you hold the stock for a certain period of time and you sell it after that period of time. Depending on how much money is involved, you might actually make more on your investment by paying capital gains tax instead of ordinary income tax.

People get tripped up on this because if you invest in stocks and you see the stock appreciate fairly quickly, your natural instinct is to lock in your profits. Most people would love to sell so they can gain a profit. When they do that, they are taxed at ordinary income tax rates. Meaning, their overall profits are calculated and they pay based on their income tax bracket. This is very different with capital gains tax. If you make a very big profit, you might actually save a lot of money paying the capital gains tax rate instead of regular ordinary income tax bracket rates.

Deferred "Income"

There are certain investments set aside by law that enjoy different tax rates. The biggest example of this is the Roth IRA in the United States. The Roth IRA enables you to buy and sell stocks with the money in your IRA account.

Knock yourself out. Keep buying stocks, selling them, and keeping the profits. When you sell, by law, you are not taxed. It's only when you withdraw or redeem money from your Roth IRA that you get taxed. This system doesn't do away with taxation altogether. Instead, it just defers the taxation to a later period.

This is a very good thing because if you are going to be buying and selling a lot of stocks to grow your overall portfolio value, you might end up paying a lower tax once you start redeeming money from your Roth IRA account. This savings can be tremendous if the value of your account is very high.

Keep these tax scenarios in mind when looking to make investments. Always factor in taxation. It's never going to go away. It's part of life and you have to make sure you plan ahead and include it in how you analyze your investment opportunities. It may turn out that after you have factored in the tax consequences of an investment, that investment might not be all that attractive after all.

Always factor in taxes, otherwise, the government might eat up quite a bit of your investment's value. You could have been investing that extra cash to grow your money even further. So a little bit of strategic planning, as far as tax consequences go, can help you safeguard and increase the value of your investment dollars.

Chapter 6: Quick Introduction to Asset Classes

Now that you have a broad idea of why you should invest as well as the tax consequences of investment and your overall risk profile as an investor, the next step is to get an overview of the things that you can put your investment money on. While it's clear to you that you want to beat inflation and preserve and grow the value of your money, at this point in time, it's probably unclear to you as to where you're going to put your money.

It's very easy to get taken in by specific investments. For example, a friend of yours tells you that she invested in Netflix. She got in at $100, and now it's at $120. Maybe she would tell you about Apple stocks and she got in at $80, and now her Apple stock is worth tens of thousands of dollars, if not, hundreds of thousands of dollars.

It's easy to get sidetracked when people talk along those terms because people get taken in by the common misconception that investments are pretty much indistinguishable from each other. If you're putting your money into stocks, then it's not really that much different from putting it in gold or precious metals or bonds. You're just buying in and hoping that the value rises and then you're cashing out. It's easy to end up comparing apples to oranges.

You probably don't need me to remind you of how foolish that is. If you're going to be making a truly informed investment decision, you have to think in terms of asset classes. An asset class is a category of investments that share certain characteristics. They invest in a specific form and they invest in a specific type of asset.

For example, real estate investment can take many different forms. You can invest in an apartment building, or you can invest in a commercial building complex or a mall. While the dollar figures and management issues involved are going to be vastly different, you're still dealing with an investment that is rooted in land. Real estate property, after all, involves land and the building structure built on top of that land.

Also, the way you make money off that structure falls within a certain range. You can rent month to month. You can ask your tenants to pay ahead of time. Maybe they would pay their lease one year in advance. Whatever the case may be, you're charging for their physical presence in your property for a certain fixed period of time. That's how it works for the real estate asset class.

Of course, there are many different variations to this, but there are certain common factors like land, structure, rent and also the taxes that arise from this activity. Compare this with a different asset class called stocks.

With stocks, you're basically buying shares of ownership in a company. You're not directly managing the company, you're not a direct partner in the company. In many cases, you don't even get the right to a share of the earnings of the company, unless the company issues a dividend. Instead, you get ownership rights. You can then sell these ownership rights or ownership stake in an aftermarket called the stock exchange.

There are many different variations to this. You can buy options to the stocks, you can buy the direct stocks itself, or you can buy stocks at IPO. Whatever the case may be, the stock asset class has certain commonalities as well.

When looking to invest, think in terms of asset classes. It's really important to make sure that you think in terms of a category that you separate all your different investment opportunities in terms of the category of investment they fall under. Why? Each asset class has different growth rates. Each asset class also has different risk profiles.

Finally, each asset class has different purchasing procedures. This means that the way you enter or buy into a particular investment asset varies from asset class to asset class. The same applies to exiting your investment or liquidating your investment.

Keep this in mind because a lot of newbie investors think that investing is as smooth, easy and fluid as investing in stocks. If it were only that easy.

Make no mistake about it, if you invest in real estate and in a partnership, for example, the entry and exit processes as well as costs are going to be different than if you were to buy stocks over the counter or at the New York stock exchange. As you can tell from all these differences among asset classes, there are specific advantages and disadvantages to each asset class. Keep this in mind.

Quick Overview

Before I go into a chapter by chapter deeper analysis of the different asset classes covered by this introduction to investing, I'm going to give you a quick overview of 4 of these asset classes.

Stocks

A stock is simply a legal ownership share or stake in a private or public company. Now, when people talk about stocks, they usually talk about shares issued by companies that are publicly traded. This is the most common perception of stock investing.

But in terms of asset class, there are other types of stocks out there. You can buy shares in a private corporation through a private placement. Also, you can buy stocks in the form of individual shares. You go to a broker, you pick out a public company and you buy shares directly.

A common alternative to this is to buy a stock through a mutual fund. In other words, you buy the mutual fund because you know that the mutual fund manager tends to buy stocks in a particular industry. Since you think that a company A, which is in industry B is going to be appreciating quite well in the future, you then buy a mutual fund C that specializes in stocks that are in industry B. Do you see how this works?

Bonds

Bonds, as mentioned earlier, are IOU's issued by the government and private corporations. It's important to understand that bonds take many different forms. This is especially true if you're buying government bonds.

There are certain tax advantages to buying bonds issued by government units. For example, if a city or a state is trying to raise money, they can issue bonds that are marketed as tax free. Private companies also issue debt obligations and these take many different forms. Either you redeem them based on a schedule or you can redeem them all at once.

Corporate bonds also have a fixed interest rate on its face. You might think that people would hang on to bonds because they are focused on getting that interest rate. Actually bonds go up and down in value and their effective yields change accordingly because of market forces.

For example, if a lot of investors start buying up the bonds of a certain company because they think that it's a very solid company, its yields actually go down. If you factor in the price that you pay for the bond against the interest rate on the bond, your actual yield might be fairly low.

The flip side is also true. If very few people are buying the bond, then the interest rate on the bonds can be quite high. These are called "junk bonds."

Real Estate

There are many different ways to invest in real estate. You can flip houses. You can go to the bank, get their list of foreclosed houses. You can get a contractor, clean up a foreclosed unit and then sell it for up to twice or more than the price you paid for it.

People do this all the time. But this is fairly low level and small scale real estate investing. It's also very active. You actually have to roll up your sleeves, pick up the phone and, at the very least, deal with contractors so they can fix up your property so you can flip it later. You also put in work to sell the property.

Other investors in real estate take a more passive approach. They would invest in pooled funds called REIT or real estate investment trust. These are like mutual funds for real estate properties. They have a lot more money to work with, so they tend to buy bigger chunks of land and bigger commercial complexes like office buildings, mall complexes or massive apartment developments.

Real estate has its own specific time line because it's not like stocks that you can quickly liquidate. Also, people can take quite a while to buy or lease real estate.

Business Partnerships

Business partnerships can be great investments. You can partner up with people who are looking for capital partners. You essentially invest your money and you play a role in the actual management of the business.

Similarly, you can become a limited partner where you put in money, but you're not actively managing the business.

Finally, you can be a member of an LLC or LLP (Limited Liability Partnership.) The great thing about this type of partnership is that you only risk the money that you invest. If that company that you're a partner in runs into legal trouble, worse comes to worst, a legal judgment will only take away your investment. They can't run after you individually and force you to sell your assets to cover the judgment. You get some legal protection with an LLP or LLC. There are also tax benefits, depending on how you structure the company.

Keep the quick overview above in mind when looking at different investment opportunities. The basic questions that you should ask yourself should go along the lines of: Which asset class is this investment opportunity in? How does this particular investment opportunity compare to other opportunities within the same asset class? Compared to benchmarked investments like an index fund tied to the Dow Jones Industrial Average or some other index, how well does this particular investment perform? Finally, what kind of tax liabilities or protections do I face if I invest in this particular investment?

You have to ask yourself these questions. Unfortunately, you won't get a solid answer unless you have a clear idea of what asset classes are.

You have to understand that when you size up different investment opportunities, you're always comparing them with each other, you're always comparing them with other classes, but you're also comparing them with other opportunities within the same asset class. This is how you get a clear picture of the overall risk profile and attractiveness of that investment opportunity.

The last thing that you want is to jump in with both feet and invest because it's supposed to be a "hot investment" or the person promoting the investment throws out a seemingly amazing percentage growth rate. You always have to keep asking yourself, how is this a good deal? Compared to what? If you fail to ask these questions, chances are quite good that you might end up with an investment that is not so hot or it might go sour faster than you think.

Chapter 7: Stock Investing: The What, Where, When, How, and Why

A lot of people wax poetic about the value of investing in stocks. In fact, a lot of people talk about stocks like it was the best thing since sliced bread. What's the big deal? As the old saying goes, "where there is smoke there is fire."

Sure there are a lot of people praising stock investing to the high heavens. There are a lot of people who are claiming that stock investing will make you rich. Well, if you look past the hype and exaggerations, there is actually quite a lot of truth in stock investing; however, it is not as exaggerated or extreme as you may be led to believe.

If you are simply looking to beat inflation at a healthy rate and look forward to a lot more money during your retirement years, stock investing is a good idea.

To put this all in context, let me tell you about Microsoft's stocks. When I first became aware of stock investing, I was just out of high school. I was working in a hardware store and a friend of mine was really big in stocks.

Microsoft at that time was trading at $100/share. I thought it was a bit high so my first instinct was to look for other cheaper stocks. These cheaper stocks in my mind had potential but didn't cost $100/share. Well, that was my first lesson in stock investing wisdom.

The golden lesson which still applies today, and I am sure will continue to apply long into the future is this: good stocks are still good stocks, regardless of how much they cost.

That $100 that I could have invested in Microsoft would have been easily worth $400-$600 now. In other words, thanks to many stock splits, as well as increases in its per share value, Microsoft is worth many times more now than when I first became aware of it.

Now what does this have to do with investing? Well, you only need to compare what my money would have been worth if I had placed it in the bank.

If you put money in the bank, you are tied to the interest rate. This is a serious problem because bank rates, including time deposits and certificates of deposits, track inflation. Put simply, if you put your money in the bank, and you are hoping that your money will grow in value due to interest, the interest is hard-wired to inflation.

For example, if the inflation rate is 5%, then you will be lucky if you can find a legitimate institutional bank that would deliver an interest rate significantly north of the inflation rate. Now to add insult to injury, whatever interest your money earned is also taxed. You see how this works? That is why a lot of people invest in the stock market. The return in investment is so much better compared to bank deposits.

The big difference between bank deposits and stocks is the fact that bank interest rates the banks are "safer" investments than stocks. I put the word the word safer in quotes because there are situations where banks fall. If you don't believe me, look up Bank of America. There are many banks that used to be flying high and seem solid that simply crashed and burned during tough economic times.

Just because you put your money in a certificate of deposit does not necessarily mean that your money will still be there tomorrow. All sorts of things can happen. However, by and large, banks tend to be safer than stocks.

40

What turns people off from stocks is the fact that stocks can be quite volatile. If something can be worth $200 today, it can easily be worth $400 next week. If you think this is crazy, look up the stock value fluctuation during the gold rush years of Internet stocks. Stocks fluctuated wildly. In fact, Amazon.com was one of those stocks that gained and lost billions of dollars in a matter of months. That is how volatile stock values are.

While it is easy to get excited when a stock is experiencing a massive upswing, it is very easy to get scared when it crashes. This is what turns a lot of people off from stocks.

What are Stocks and How do they Work?

Stocks are shares of ownership in a company. All corporations have shareholders. However, most corporations in the United States and elsewhere are private. When there is a public market for the buying and selling of stocks, the stocks are what are called publicly traded stocks. The company is then called a "public company".

When a company offers shares to the public, it only does so pretty much one time. This is called an initial public offering. You are letting the public know that they can buy ownership shares of the company. Now, after the IPO, what takes place is a secondary market. This is where people who bought shares of the company, buy and sell shares among others who are interested in the company.

In terms of the company actually getting money from the public, this is done through the IPO. The IPO is crucial because it puts a dollar value on the shares owned by all shareholders. They may not have released their shares to the public for sale during the IPO; they can release shares over time.

Still, when they do that, they are engaged in the secondary market. Because only during the initial public offering is the company directly selling shares to the public. This has the effect of pricing the shares of all the shareholders. Now, keep in mind that in some cases, companies can also do a secondary public offering. This is kind of a misnomer because what they do is they would take the public price of the stock, or the price on which the stock is trading and then use it as a benchmark for the secondary issuance of shares.

The idea behind public companies is for corporations tap a large market of investors looking to buy ownership. The investors may not necessarily get dividends. Back in the day, corporations who went public issue dividends. They would split up the profit that the company made among all the shareholders based on the shares owned by the shareholders.

This is no longer the case. There are many high-value corporations that don't issue dividends but are still worth a lot of money. Investors primarily buy stocks for the growth in the value of their shares. They don't generally buy stocks because of dividend returns. While a dividend is a good thing, it is definitely welcome.

How does Stock Trading Work?

Once a stock is issued, there are companies called market makers who have rights to stocks that they haven't sold yet, or they have bought these shares directly during the IPO or anytime thereafter. These market makers essentially ensure that there are shares that the public can buy.

The shares are traded through a bid and ask system. Generally, the bid price for a stock is lower than the amount asked for by the owner or the market maker. This may all seem confusing because you probably have ideas of a room full of people holding up their hands and signaling to each other how much they want to buy and sell stocks.

Well, that is how it used to be. Now thanks to digital trading, this is all done electronically in split seconds. Stock values can fluctuate and bid and ask pricing are dynamically adjusted based on volume as well as how much people are willing to bid for a share of a stock.

This is also decentralized. While stock markets share central platforms that do the trading, in terms of systems that do the actual trading, the decisions are decentralized. It's no longer the case where all decisions are made in New York or London. Instead, traders from all over the world using their computers can make decisions, and this is relayed in real time to the central electronic trading system.

This is the reason why a lot of trading platforms are getting cheaper. You used to have to hire a stockbroker and pay hefty fees just to buy and sell stocks, not anymore. You only need to create an account with an online broker, and you are good to go. The broker has all the necessary connections and memberships to all the platforms, and you can start trading away.

The Advantages of Stocks

Believe it or not, the big advantage of stocks is precisely its volatility. Unlike bank deposits which ties you to a very low return for years, stocks can go up quite a bit assuming that you pick the right company.

There are many examples of biotechnology companies that were trading for pennies or nearly pennies per share. Once their FDA approval goes through, their stock value explodes. It is not unheard of for a biotechnology company to trade for less than a dollar or even pennies on the dollar to hit several dozen dollars worth of value per share.

Volatility in this context is very welcome indeed. However, you have to have the risk profile and risk appetite for it. Again, it is easy to get excited when a stock is going up and your $1 turns to $2 or even $5. It is another matter entirely when your $1 turns into $0.20 or $0.10. This is entirely possible with stocks.

Now the good news a large chunk of stocks is not this volatile. There are certain sectors and industries that are very volatile, but there are others that tend to track sideways or appreciate sideways.
For example, utilities tend to be fairly stable. The bad news is they don't have much of an upside as other stocks, however, if you are scared of losing your shirt in the stock market, then you can at least be rest assured that they won't tank overnight.

Extreme Liquidity

Another key advantage of stocks as an asset class is the fact that it is very liquid. You can buy stocks one day and decide to liquidate your whole position. You don't have to wait months like in real estate. You don't have to fill out a form like with a bank deposit. You just go online and execute a trade. Depending upon the trading platform that you use, you can get real time value so you can lock in on gains fairly quickly.

This liquidity is very attractive because you can quickly move in and out of those stocks very easily. Of course, this depends on the kind of stocks that you buy.

When people think of trading in the stock market, they usually think about shares traded through the New York Stock Exchange and NASDAQ. However, if you look at the total stock market in the United States, there is actually quite a diversity. There are pink sheets, which are electronically traded penny stocks. There are OTC bullets and board (OTCBB) stocks that also tend to be penny stocks. Of course, the more obscure the platform, the higher the risk you take.

The good news is, with stocks and investments in general, the higher the risks, the higher the reward. There is a reason why risky stocks tend to deliver handsome returns. That is how the market is set up.

People who invest in risky assets demand a higher return. In stocks, this plays out when a lot of the initial risk that is involved takes place when the stock goes through its developmental stage. The risk is shouldered by the initial buyers. These are people who buy in for pennies on the dollar.

However, once it becomes increasingly clear that the company is actually going to turn a profit or going to get its FDA application for a new drug approved, more institutional or traditional investors come in. These then start buying up the stocks of the initial risk takers. Put simply, as the overall risk profile of a stock goes from extremely risky to moderate or even non-risky, the price increases and stabilizes. This is a golden opportunity for initial risk takers. They took the risk that is why they got that nice return.

Managing Risks

As you can probably already tell from the description of stock investing that it can be very risky. While it is easy to get excited about buying a stock for $0.50, and then seeing your $0.50 turning into $8 or even $80, the sad reality is that most people don't manage to pull off such returns. While it does happen, it happens quite rarely.

In most cases, the stock investors' returns tend to be more conservative. We are talking about less than 20% annually. If they are pushing it, maybe they can hit 33% year on year portfolio value growth. The reason why most people are unable to achieve such spectacular returns is due to risk management. Unless you are sure, you don't really care if you see your initial investment dollars come back. It makes a lot of sense for you to manage risks.

Risk management in stocks is pretty straightforward. You can diversify based on the stocks you buy, or you can diversify based on industry. The whole point of diversification is when you have your eggs in many different baskets, even if several of those baskets get dropped and your eggs destroyed, you still have eggs left in other baskets. They still have a chance to grow in value.

By the same token, when you diversify based on industry, you are placing an educated bet that some industries are more stable than others. For example, the Internet industry is known for wild fluctuations of value; that is how Internet stocks behave. They can go up a lot for several months and then when a bad earnings report comes out, their stock could tank. That is how volatile they could be.

As I mentioned earlier, there are certain stocks like utility stocks that are fairly stable. The downside with those stocks is that you don't get that nice pumped up feeling that you get with Internet stocks, but at the very least, you can stay in the middle of an acceptable portfolio growth rate year after year. Diversifying based on industry is a tried and proven way of managing your risks when investing in stocks.

You can also diversify based upon the type of stocks you buy. In other words, you can be invested all in one industry, but you spread out your exposure to that industry among different players. This is very important because not all companies within an industry perform equally well. Some are managed very competently. Others are reeling from the consequences of past management's bad decisions. Every company has a different story, that is why they perform differently.

There is also the impact upon the fortunes of the overall industry. When you diversify within an industry, you basically spread out your risk among the different companies there. This way, the better run companies that are rewarded by the market tend to equalize the stagnation or even outright losses you experience betting on companies that aren't doing so well.

Manage your Risks through Pooled Investments

The big downside to investing in stocks directly is time management. You might not have the time you need to learn all you need to learn about a particular industry, or to weigh different stocks and see which ones are worth investing in.

Unfortunately, this is the kind of information that can make or break your foray into stock investing. If you play the game wrong, your investment might track sideways. In other words, it might not appreciate all that much. The rest of the market is going to leave you behind.

Most people don't have the experience as well as the training needed to become excellent stock pickers. Now don't get me wrong, there are individual investors who get the knack of stock investing and, more often than not, they are right as far as their stock choices go. However, those people are relatively rare. If you are the typical investor, you probably don't have the time nor patience to learn what you need to learn to do a consIstent job of picking stock winners.

This is where mutual funds come in. Mutual funds are essentially pooled investments where you pay a professional fund manager for his or her expertise to pick stocks. You can then rest assured that the person has properly diversified either within an industry or among several industries.

Also, several mutual funds have its own particular focus. Some mutual funds are very risky. They tend to invest in emerging markets' stocks. Others tend to be more conservative. You can diversify your stock investment portfolio by diversifying among the different mutual funds out there because they do have different risk profile expertise.

Individual Stock Investing vs Pooled Investment

As I mentioned above, unless you have a lot of time, it is probably a good idea to initially invest in mutual funds. You can use your exposure to mutual funds to acclimate yourself with stock investing. Once you have achieved a certain level of expertise, you can then start investing in individual stocks.

Now the big difference between investing in mutual funds and investing in individual stocks is the return that you get. Mutual funds are diversified. So even though it appreciates in value, it doesn't appreciate in value as dramatically and as quickly than if you invested in individual stocks directly.

For example, if you were to put all your stock investment funds into Netflix stock, you will be sitting pretty right now because Netflix experienced an explosive growth in stock value in recent years.

However, when individual stocks pan out, unfortunately the chances of this happening for people who are not professional stock investors or stock fund managers, is relatively low. There is a little bit of a survivor bias going on here because everybody gets all excited about the bets that made it. We all hear about the amazing stories of people turning $1 to $10, everybody gets excited about that.

It is also worth noting that for every winner, there are probably many more losers we just don't hear about. It's not like somebody is going to make a big deal of the fact that he or she lost hundreds of thousands of dollars in the stock market buying the wrong individual stocks.

Accordingly, if you are just really trying your hand with stock investing, you might want to go with mutual funds first. Besides the risks mentioned above, another downside of individual stocks is the cost of diversification.

With mutual funds, you are pretty much automatically diversified, not so with individual stocks. You have to make the diversification call yourself and you might not have all that much money with which to diversify.

The bottom line is simple. When you deal with pooled investments, pooled funds mean more diversification and you are assured of more expert management.

A Quick Word About Mutual Funds

I wish I could tell you that all mutual funds are created equal, but they are not. They are managed by experts. They are experts primarily because they know more than you do. However, that may not be saying much. Not all mutual funds do well.
While many tend to outperform at the same level as the general market, and quite a number tend to outperform, there is also a large number of mutual funds that underperform the market.

For example, the market appreciates at an annual rate of 12%-18%. You might get stuck with a mutual fund that barely grows at 8%. Just because you invest in a mutual fund does not necessarily mean you are locked in at a certain rate of appreciation.

How do you prevent getting stuck in the wrong fund? First, you need to pay attention to its track record. Keep in mind that past track record does not predict future performance. If you have looked at all sorts of mutual fund brochures, this would be plainly stated at the bottom. They would have a chart, and it would say, "past performance does not indicate future performance." This is true.

Nevertheless, having a track record is better than not having one. You can tell from how the fund manager makes certain investment decisions, whether these decisions lead to more positive results or not. This is much better than simply being asked to take a massive risk on a fund that just launched. It has no track record. You don't know how good its fund managers' decisions are. You operate completely in the dark.

Accordingly, you need to look at the different mutual funds that you are considering and pay attention to their past performance. Look at their performance on an annual basis as well as on a quarterly basis.

Another key factor you need to consider when sizing up many different mutual funds is how "fast" their appreciation is. Some mutual funds are notoriously slow. In fact, they have become bureaucratized.

Now that does not mean that you should automatically avoid them. Many very "slow" funds are worth billions of dollars, and they barely match the performance of the market as a whole. For most investors, this is good enough. Why? The bigger the asset base of the mutual fund, the more resources it has to at least try to match the market. If you are just looking to perform fairly evenly with the market or slightly outperform it, then bigger funds are for you.

However, if you are younger, and you have a larger risk appetite, and a more risk friendly profile, such mutual fund may be too slow for you. You would be better off looking for mutual funds that are marketed as aggressive.

Now pay attention to how that mutual fund actually performs. It's one thing for a fund to be marketed as "aggressive." It is another for it to truly produce aggressive results. Now, when I mention the word "aggressive," don't get too excited. A lot of people think that if a fund is aggressive, the returns are just phenomenal. This is not necessarily the case.

A mutual fund may be aggressive going up; it may be aggressive going down. In other words, it is aggressive taking the risks. It is another matter entirely whether the risk taken produces the intended results.

The Advantages of Mutual Funds

To recap, mutual funds can be quite advantageous because your money is being professionally managed. It is not like the person managing the fund just got out of college. The fund managers tend to be seasoned veterans. They tend to have a general idea of how the markets will work and how certain stock buys will end up.

Next, when you buy into mutual funds, you are buying into a large pool of assets. This enables the fund manager to buy a lot more stock. The volume buying can have a positive effect on the stock's overall appreciation rate. Because as more and more institutional buyers buy up a stock, other institutional buyers would pay attention, and this can produce a larger appreciation rate, or at the least, a more sustainable one.

Compare this with buying into a stock that is sustained primarily by individual buyers. In that scenario, you are at the mercy of the hype and excitement surrounding a particular stock. Good luck to you when that excitement dries up. If you need a concrete example of this, look up many Dot Com companies that were flying high right before the Dot Com crashed. A large chunk of them was hit and too many of those were unable to recover. They either completely disappeared, or they got swallowed, or they are now a tiny shell of what they used to be.

The Disadvantages of Mutual Funds

The big disadvantage of mutual funds is that diversification tends to dampen gains. For example, if a stock manager buys ten companies, and two of those companies are outperforming the market like gang busters, but four of those companies are under performing like crazy, the overall average gain might be nothing to write home about. In other words, whatever you could have gained if you bought those winning stocks individually were more than offset by under performing stocks.

Another key sticking point with mutual funds involves the issue of management costs. Many mutual funds charge a fee the moment you buy into the fund. This is called the front-loaded fund. Others charge when you are redeeming your asset. This is all well and good. A fee is a fee, and it shouldn't really matter if it is charged at the front or made at the end.

The bigger issue is how the costs are calculated. Some mutual funds charge management costs even if the fund lost money. I hope you can see why this irritates some investors because it is like adding insult to injury.

Finally, a big disadvantage some investors see in mutual funds is that it can be quite slow in locking in profits. In other words, a mutual fund might buy a stock that is really hot and blows up in value, and then only get to unload that stock once its value has crashed to normal levels.

In other words, the mutual fund never really fully realized the massive short-term gain from the stock. This is because mutual funds tend to buy stocks in huge blocks, and this can get in the way of them locking in profits through quick entry and quick exit.

If you were buying stocks individually, you can do this. You can buy a stock right before it pops, and then you can put in a stop limit order at a certain peak price. Once it hits that peak price, you are out of the stock.

In fact, this is programmed in so you don't have to necessarily monitor the stock price in real time, you can do this while you are sleeping. You just simply set up the stop limit right after you buy, and you are good to go.

This is how many individual investors lock in on anything from a 2% to 15% return on investment.

Investment Costs

When you are investing in stocks, your primary costs take two forms. First is the platform costs. This is not a surprise. All trading platforms will tell you flat out how much they charge per transaction. Whether you are buying, or you are selling, there will be a cost.

The second cost that you need to be mindful of involves taxes. In the United States, if you are buying and selling stocks very rarely within a year, let's say you buy a stock, and then you hold onto it for more than a year; you are only taxed at a capital gains tax rate.

However, if you buy and sell stocks regularly, your tax rate is the same as your regular income rate. You have to adjust the accounting of your profits and losses accordingly, there is a tremendous tax consequence when you choose to account for losses and gains in your stock trading.

With mutual funds, the cost of buying into a fund is pretty straightforward. There is a cost charged by the fund, and there is also a cost charged by the platform you use to buy your position in the fund.

In terms of internal costs mentioned above, you have to look at the prospectus of the mutual fund you are thinking of buying because the fund management may be basing their funds on the net value instead of net profit, or net year on year appreciation.

Moreover, there are some mutual funds that are notorious for charging a very high rate for management fees. This is all well and good if the fund manager is some sort of superstar and can almost guarantee amazing returns. This is definitely going to be a problem if the fund manager is quite mediocre and the fund either barely keeps up with market performance or flat out under performs.

Chapter 8: Investing in Real Estate

If stocks seem like a bit of a gamble to you, there is a pretty solid alternative in the form of real estate.

One reservation some people have against stock trading is the fact that you are investing in something that is not really tangible. You are investing in shares of ownership. Now, it is a little more tangible if the company actually issues dividends. Dividend-paying public companies actually give you a share of the actual after-tax profits of the company.

However, these companies are the minority. The vast majority of companies that trade at NASDAQ or the New York Stock Exchange do not issue dividends. You're essentially buying a right to ownership which you can then freely buy and sell.

Some people think that this is too intangible. They are looking for something more "real"; this is where real property comes in.

When you buy real property, you are buying land or legal access to land in the form of a long-term lease. Real estate for many people is "solid investment" because it is something you can see. For example, if you buy a partnership share in a real estate partnership, there is an actual building or an actual collection of homes or rental properties. Whatever the case may be, you can go to a specific point on the map that contains the object that you have an ownership stake in.

This is not necessarily the case with stocks. In theory, you can look at Apple Computer's space-age headquarters and say that you are a part-owner. If you own Apple stocks, you are a part-owner of that building but the feeling of ownership is not the same as if you had a physical building you can point to.

Besides the optics and its psychological effects, real estate investing also has its key advantages that many people throughout history have sought.

What is Real Estate and Why should You Invest in it?

Real estate may seem like an investment class that deals with land and buildings on top of the land. This is not always the case. When you invest in real estate, you may not necessarily be buying land per se. Although you can buy land, real estate investing is a broad term that also covers long-term leases.

In other words, you don't own the land forever. The owner of the land may have leased it to you for 20 years or 50 years. Furthermore, you then get the right to put structures on the land, as well as charge people to stay in the structure for a fixed period of time.

Real estate investment is fairly broad because it covers a wide range of activities. What they all have in common is that they all have something to do with the land itself or the rights that flow from having the legal authority to be on that piece of land.

Also, real estate is very broad. When people think of real property, they think of a house and a lot, or an office building, but it is actually much broader than that. It can be a commercial space. It can be an apartment complex. It can be a mall. It can be an office building, and so on and so forth.

The reason why a lot of people invest in real estate is simple economics. While the global population reliably increases year after year, the supply of land remains the same. Given this reality, real estate can be a winning proposition.

Now, I say the words "can be a winning proposition" because there are certain historical time frames where investing in real estate is a losing proposition. You only need to look at the great Financial Crash of 2008 to see this in action.

Back in 2008, due to the credit crunch, lots of real estate properties went through foreclosure. Real estate values throughout almost all the United States sank, not anymore.

After the economy recovered, real estate is now showing its historical growth patterns. Generally speaking, real estate appreciates in value year after year, again thanks to the disparity between population growth and zero growth of available land.

Another advantage to real estate is it can become a quite passive form of investment. For example, if you buy an apartment complex, and you hire a property management company to collect your rent, to make the necessary repair, and to deal with tenants, you pretty much have recurring income that you don't have to actively work for.

Every single month, rent money comes in. After the property management comes in and takes out their fees and costs, what you have left is your income. You did not actively work for it. You did not have to hassle for it. It just comes. You earn money in your sleep. This is passive income.

If you want to make your real estate venture as passive as possible, you can take things up a notch by doing business with a real estate development company. The company just leases the land from you and pays you an annual lease fee. It does everything else. It does the development. It recruits tenants. It collects from the tenants. It maintains the structures, so on and so forth. However, year after year, you just get the lease payments from the company.

In fact, in many situations, the real estate development company will pay you the lease many years in advance. Talking about passive, that is why real estate has historically been quite popular.

In fact, in many cultures, the real definition of a truly "rich person" or a "wealthy person" is whether this person owns land. Even to this very day, there are many cultures that define wealth primarily in terms of land.

Now this doesn't mean they are clueless about other forms of wealth. It is not as if they have not heard of bond investing, but they still prefer real estate holdings because of its passive nature. You just get the legal right to that piece of property and depending on how you work with partners or developers. Your real estate holdings can actually produce a purely passive income where the only work that you need to do is to go to the bank to cash your check.

Real Estate vs Stocks

An asset class' value doesn't exist within a vacuum. It only has value when you compare it to something else. Accordingly, when trying to come up with a realistic assessment of the value of real estate, you have to compare it with stocks. How does real estate measure up to stocks?
Well, if you are looking for massive growth rates, you are probably better off investing in companies of speculative industries or speculative stocks. However, if you are looking for steady appreciation in value, and you want an asset that would always be worth something, you might want to consider taking a long hard look at real estate.

The great thing about real estate is that it will always be worth something. As I mentioned above, there was a great Financial Crash of 2008 where a lot of real estate properties sank in value, but they never went to zero. They were still worth something. The good news is if the location where the real estate property is located recovers, its market value will go up; you are not starting from zero.

Compare this with stocks. There are many cases of stocks starting out worth $200 or more and after the industry crash is resolved, the stock is not worth pennies. You only have to look up Dot Com companies in the early 2000s to see what I am talking about.

It's crazy, but you don't get that nightmare scenario with real estate. The real estate that you buy will always be worth something, whether it is going to be worth something more than you paid for is another discussion. Keep in mind that real estate prices are very localized. That is why the number one rule in real estate is: location, location, location.

You cannot compare real estate that you buy in San Francisco with real estate that you buy in Montana. It just does not work. You are comparing apples to oranges. Still, the fact that investors get a stable "bottom" with real estate is very reassuring for many investors. These are usually risk averse investors or investors who have a fairly low tolerance to risks.

Another key difference between real estate and stocks involves appreciation. While asset prices in real estate do appreciate, and in many cases quite significantly, the rate of appreciation is not as volatile as with stocks. When a local area goes up in value, it keeps going up.

You know that there is a problem with the market once that growth rate starts to slow down. That is how you can tell that the real estate market in that particular situation is cooling.

This is not the case with stocks. When a stock is hot, it can go up in value tremendously, like 2% -10% per day. If it reaches its run, there is a pullback, and it can come crashing down to a much lower price than when it began its climb.

Depending on your risk profile, this can be a good thing or bad thing for investors who are very risk tolerant. The relatively slow appreciation of real estate values may be an experience similar to watching grass grow. I can get annoying very quickly. However, for investors who have a very low tolerance to risk, that is precisely the kid of growth rate they are happy with. The massive upswings and downswings of stocks may be too much for them.

The Pros and the Cons of Real Estate Investing

So what are the advantages and disadvantages of investing in real estate? Well, the first one big advantage is you are assured, absent extraordinary times like the 2008 Financial Crash that your property will always go up in value. It might not be much on a year to year average, but there might be some spikes.

The reason why you can get this sense of assurance is there is a limited inventory of land. It is not like there are new planets being discovered and human beings are colonizing that planet, freeing up a huge new inventory of land. Our land inventory here on planet Earth is fixed, while at the same time, our population growth rate is increasing.

Another key advantage of real estate investing is that it is more open to passive income. You really can't say that your stock portfolio is passive income because there is no income unless you cash out. It's anyone's guess when you will cash out because you might get stuck in a situation where you are waiting for the price to go back up so you can turn a profit when you exit the stock, not so with real estate.

If you buy the right kind of real estate, you can get a purely passive income. You can partner with a development company that would lease your land and send you a check year after year. They will do all the hard work. They do all the sweating for you. They find the tenants. They deal with problem tenants. They make developments. They build the necessary buildings. They apply for the necessary permits, so on down the line. Your only job is to receive the check and encash it.

Another advantage of real estate property is they are "real." Your wealth is tangible. You can say to people, "I own that building" or "I own that district in that city." When they go there, sure enough, they see something.

This is not the case with stocks. With stocks, all you really get is a right to trade in a certain amount of shares of ownership in stock. That is all you are getting; you get pieces of paper. Stock ownership is more "real" if the company is issuing a dividend but as I mentioned previously, this is no longer the case. This is not done as a matter of course.

Disadvantages of Real Estate

Unfortunately, there is no such thing as a perfect investment asset and real estate has its fair share of disadvantages. In fact, some of these disadvantages are such turnoffs to investors that they don't bother with real estate at all. Real estate is a non-issue with them. Again, it all depends on your risk profile, how much money you have and your time frame.

First, it takes considerable capital to invest in real estate. Unless you are investing in an REIT, which is like a vehicle for buying into real estate properties, direct real estate investment can cost a pretty penny. At the very least, you need to take out a loan from the bank.

Even if the bank is going to be footing the vast majority of the acquisition cost of your real estate holdings, you are still responsible for the down payment. Now depending on the kind of loan that you are getting, this can be as high as north of 20%. If you are buying a multi-million dollar property, this is going to be a problem since most people does not have a few million bucks lying around.

The second big disadvantage with real estate is that it is not very liquid. While you can make quite a nice paper profit on your real estate holdings, realizing that paper profit can take quite some time.

For example, you can get an assessment done on the fair market value of properties surrounding your own property. You might get a very nice price estimate from the appraiser. However, that value is not money in the bank unless, and until you liquidate your property, or you rent out that property for that fair market value rent that was reported to you.

Now knowing the value of something is one thing, actually getting that value is another matter entirely. At the very least, you are going to have to wait. You are going to have to put up a sign saying, "this property is for sale" or "this property is for lease." It is anybody's guess when you will have a buyer or a new tenant.

Compare this with stocks. If you see the current value is $50, you can log into your online stockbroker account, click a few buttons, and you have exited your stock position for $50 a share minus the fee that you pay. This is called liquidity.

Stocks always have ready buyers, not so with real estate. Sure your property might be worth a lot of money, but it's only a theoretical value until and unless somebody comes up and pulls out his dollars to buy or lease the property.

Another downside to real estate property involves local market realities. The great thing about stocks is there is a national or global stock valuation system, called the market. It is not like a share of Amazon is worth less to investors in Russia, compared to investors in the Philippines. It does not work that way.

Regardless on where you are on the planet, if you want to buy Amazon stocks, you are going to have to pay the current real time stock value of Amazon stock, very straightforward, no mysteries about it, no need to have connections. It is all very transparent; n so with real estate. Real estate may have a local fair market value, but its value actually fluctuates based on local market realities.

Even if you live in the same city, let us say Los Angeles, certain parts of Los Angeles have higher appreciation rates, while others continue to remain stagnant or under perform the market. That is just on the citywide level.

You can take things to a different level if you compare city to city. There is a big difference with local real estate valuations between Bakersfield, California and San Francisco, California. It is not even close. On top of all of this, price fluctuations and price patterns vary from city to city, region to region, and even district to district.

These are a lot of price fluctuations for control for. This is a lot to stay on top of because you might be hanging on to real estate that might be dragging down your investment portfolio. You might be better off liquidating a property located in a certain district and buying up another lot in a nearby district of the city, or another district entirely because its value appreciation trajectory is much more attractive.

Finally, with real estate you are dependent on local and regional economic and political forces. While it is true that stocks are also subject to political and economic trends, this is particularly pronounced for real estate. For example, if you bought commercial property or office property in a city that announced that it is going to be the new home of a massive

Japanese multinational corporation, you can bet that that announcement will have a nice positive effect on the value of your property.

Now imagine that situation being reversed. What if you have a property in a city that is de-industrializing, or facing severe economic challenges like Detroit, Michigan? In that case, the reverse is true. The property is worth very little now. You can bet that it will be probably worth less in the future. It won't be completely worthless, but it would be worth less.

You see how this works? A lot of investors stay clear of real estate because of these issues. The good news is that REITs enabled investors to get all the benefits of real estate investing while getting the advantages of dealing in stock. Put simply, when you invest in REIT, the company issues units to the public. These units go up and down in value. The underlying asset of course involves real estate. Technically speaking, you get the best from both worlds.

Now, whether this actually pans out depends on the particular REIT that you buy. REITs offer a great way of diversifying your portfolio by adding a real estate element to it without getting your hands "dirty" with actually dealing with real estate.

As you can well imagine my explanation above, when you buy real estate, it can be a messy affair. You'd have to go to the location. You have to buy depending on how you plan to manage it. It can be quite a headache. You have to deal with a contractor, get the building built; you need to work with a property management company and on and on it goes.

When you invest in REIT that deals with malls or shopping spaces, all those headaches go away. Instead, you can look forward to the point in time when local market conditions push up the value of local real estate and rents and this then has a positive effect on the income of REIT.

Higher income translates to higher per unit share value of the REIT. That is how a lot of investors play the real estate market— through REITs.

You can still invest in real estate through individual deals, but be forewarned. It can take up quite a lot of time and whatever returns you might get might not be worth the hassle.

The Pros and Cons of REITs

There are many publicly traded REITs out there, and the big advantage of REITs is that they provide you with much-needed liquidity. Comparing getting rid of a REIT position to listing and selling a real estate property is not even close. It is not even in the same ballpark. With REIT, you can just log in to your online trading broker's platform and place an order to buy or sell. Done deal.

On the other hand, if you deal with real estate directly, you would have to list it. You have to wait for some time. You also have to deal with real estate agents and the whole ball of wax. It can be a nightmare. It can be a headache.

However, things can also be quite smooth but my point is that there is some risk there. It may not be as quick and easy as you imagined.

Chapter 9: Investing in Bonds

People, who bought internet stocks in the late 90s all the way to 2001, thought that they were buying something really valuable. In fact, a lot of them paid top dollar for their stocks. Some internet companies were trading at north of $200 per share. It was really a crazy time.

When the dot-com crash came, for every Yahoo, eBay, or Amazon that survived the slaughter, there were many more companies that didn't. These companies either became penny stocks, or they delisted. They ceased to exist. The dot-com crash is a good reminder of one central fact of stock investment. When you invest in stocks, your investment might do so badly that it may be worth zero, or nearly zero dollars.

That is the risk you take with stocks. There's no government agency you can run to give you your money back if there's no fraud involved. If the company was just badly run, or there was just a change in the economy, or things just didn't work out, your stock would be worth precisely zero or nearly zero. It doesn't matter how much money you spent on the stock initially, it doesn't matter how hard you work for your money, none of that matters. That's the reality of stock investing. You can lose your shirt.

Now, you can also look at the upside. The upside is you can buy stocks that may be $17, and a few weeks after they debuted can then be worth over $100. I am, of course, talking about Facebook stocks.

Facebook, when it first launched, had a lot of hype and the stock quickly tanked close to just north of $17. As of this writing, its fortunes have improved and sure enough, the market has rewarded its stockholders by valuing the stock at well over $100. That's how stock investing works. It's a risk. You are buying into the ownership of the company and as an owner, you take all the risks involved.

For many people, this is too much risk. They'd rather deal with public companies in the form of loans. Make no mistake about it, public companies also need to take out loans. Expanding a company takes money. Implementing a development plan requires capital. Accordingly, companies have been borrowing money from the public for a long time. This is called the bond market.

A bond is a legal obligation on the company's part to not only pay back the money that it borrowed, but pay it back at a certain interest rate. The interest is usually stated in the bond itself. People who are looking for a more "sure fire way" to invest their capital to lock in some gains invest in bonds. You are basically buying a debt instrument that was originally issued by the company.

Now, the interesting thing about bonds is that while the company has issued this debt originally and has gotten money from that debt, the holders of that debt buy and sell this debt. This is called the bond market. The same dynamic with stock trading applies. When a company issues a bond to the public, it does it generally only once. While there are secondary bond offerings, for the most part, when the company borrows money, it's a one-time thing.

What happens next to financial companies who then buy and sell these bonds? The interest rates of the bonds are the same, but the value of the bond goes up and down depending on the demand for the bond. This is called a yield. When a bond is very unpopular, its yield tends to be quite high because people are not buying up the bond. You're getting the full interest rate noted on the bond.

Now, if the company behind the bond is very solid and there is a tremendous demand for that company's loan, then the situations reverse. The yield crashes because the price of the bond increases. In other words, while the interest rate of the bond is the same, if you factor in how much money you have to pay to get the right to be paid that interest, your yield is actually quite small.

People play the bond market pretty much like stocks. You are buying bonds in hopes that they would appreciate in value over time. However, unlike stocks, which are open-ended because you can hang on to the ownership of the stock, technically speaking, forever, with bonds, there is a fixed life for the obligation. All bonds have an expiration date. While companies do issue 30 year bonds, these bonds still expire at the end of 30 years.

The Different Types of Bonds

The different classifications of bonds really depend on who issues them. Again, these are debt instruments released by an entity to the general public. The general public then essentially becomes lenders or creditors to the borrowing entity. Now, the entity can be a public company, it can be a private company, it can be a government, like a city or a municipality, it can be the national government.

Now, the type of bond also impacts its tax status. Generally speaking, interest income is taxable. Accordingly, if you buy a public company's bond, for example, General Motors, whatever interest General Motors pays you is taxable. Now, if the issuer of the bond is a government, like a municipal government or a state government, in certain situations, these bonds can be tax-free. There are many tax-free muni bonds available on the market. Whatever interest you earn is not taxed.

Advantages of Investing in Bonds

The great thing about investing in bonds is that you are buying something "more tangible" than ownership shares. According to U.S. federal law, when a company is facing financial problems, its creditors are the first priority. Since you own a loan instrument to the company, you are a creditor. If the company is going to be facing possible bankruptcy or restructuring, you are first in line.

Of course, there is another entity ahead of you, but that entity's identity is never publicly stated. However, in legal terms, the government always takes precedence. So in the off chance, the issuing corporation has to sell off its assets, as a bondholder, you have a more superior right than the stockholders of that company. In many cases, they're left with nothing. You at least have a chance of getting cents on the dollar.

This added security is what attracts a lot of people to bond investment. Another big advantage of bonds is that if you specialize in certain types of bonds, you don't have to pay tax on the interest income of those bonds. Again, these are usually municipal or government bonds.

The Disadvantage of Investing in Bonds

The big disadvantage of investing in bonds is that you trade in a lot for the assurance of the payout. There is a payout when you buy a bond. The company that issues the bonds says that it will pay a certain interest. If the company is solid, that promise is good as gold. You will get that interest.

Now, the problem here is if the interest is below the inflation rate. This does happen. Also, if you compare the rate of return you get from the debt instrument compared to the rate of the appreciation of the stock of the underlying company, you may come up behind. Do you see how this works?

Also, bonds have different ratings. The most trusted bonds, and these are the ones that hold their value the most and are the most prized, which tends to depress their yield, are government bonds. These are bonds issued by the government that are in tip-top financial shape like Japanese bonds.

On the other side of the equation are bonds issued by companies that may not be struggling, but are considered by the market to be risky. This is how the term "junk bonds" came about. Unless a company has a triple-A rating, a certain grade will get you down to junk bond status.

Junk bonds have a silver lining. Since they're considered by the market to be riskier than "safer" bonds, their yields tend to be higher. While it is a big deal when a company defaults on its bond obligations, the good news is that for the most part, when you invest in junk bonds, your investment is relatively safe. It's all comparative. It's not like companies that issue junk bonds go belly up all the time. Still, if you are looking for fairly nice rates of return, consider riskier bonds.

Bond Funds

Bond funds are mutual funds that do not yield with stock. They just buy bonds. Some of the biggest retirement funds invest in bond funds. It's easy to see why. When you invest in bonds, you're investing in debt. The company issued debt and they are legally obligated to pay it back. So at that level, bonds are safer than stocks.

Bond funds specialize in certain types of bonds. There are bond funds that invest only in the safest bonds. These are triple-A rated bonds issued by the government.

Other bond funds are more aggressive and risky. They invest in junk bonds primarily because they're looking for higher yields. Still, the underlying philosophy is the same. When bond funds buy funds, they are buying debt instruments which give them a far superior legal right to the assets of the company should things go wrong.

This is very different from a mutual fund that buys the stock of the company. If the company goes belly up, the mutual fund gets nothing, just like with all other shareholders, except possibly preferred shareholders that are given a legal first right to the company's assets right after creditors.

The big advantage of bond funds, just like with mutual funds, is that they are hiring a professional to buy bonds for you. This person buys funds in mass. This person has a solid experience dealing with the bond market. The downside to bond funds is fairly the same as mutual funds. You might get stuck with a bond fund that tracks the performance of other bond funds.

Chapter 10: Investing in Business Partnerships

Believe it or not corporations are not the only money-making enterprises in the United States. While it may seem like a lot of the big businesses in the United States and elsewhere are corporations, this is not the case. It may seem like a lot of the most successful enterprises have an "Inc." at the end of their formal business names, there are also a large number of affluent businesses that are partnerships.

If you are trying to grow the value of your money through investing, you might want to consider investing in business partnerships. This is not as well publicized as corporate investments, but partnerships also have their fair share of medium-sized to large companies. Indeed, whether a business is a corporation, a partnership or a sole proprietorship, the legal form of the business should not be confused with its success as an enterprise.

In fact, there are many very successful multi-million dollar companies that are owned by LLCs. These are limited liability companies in the US Federal Tax Code. It is important to note that due to certain requirements of particular business forms like corporations, many entrepreneurs opt to establish partnerships instead of starting a corporation in which they take on shareholders. You might want to consider investing in a business partnership if you are confident in the entrepreneurial capabilities of the people forming such partnerships.

How Business Partnerships Work

A partnership legal form is at a certain kind of misleading. Usually when people think of "partnership," they think about two people doing equal work. For example, one partner would handle the sales and marketing;

and another partner would take care of product development, manufacturing as well as internal processes. This is the classic popular picture of how partnerships work.

However, reality does not quite match this picture. In many cases, partnerships involve quite a number of people but only one or two actually operate the partnership. In other words, the active partners are very few. While other people have a share in the profits generated by the enterprise, the actual day-to-day operations are in the hands of very few people.

Generally speaking, a business partnership works this way: The partners form the company, and they pool money together that the company uses for its operations. Once the company starts generating revenues, operation costs are taken out of the revenue and whatever is left, the profits, are distributed based on the percentage ownership of the partners. Each partner takes a share of the profits. The same investment principle applies: you invest a certain amount, and you try to get back more than you put in. In other words, you are growing your money. Of course, whether you are actually able to pull that off depends on the enterprise you invest in.

Business partnerships are really no different than other businesses using other legal forms. They require good management to turn a profit. They require proper planning to remain viable for a long period of time. The only difference really is the legal form a business partnership takes. There is, however, one crucial difference that can be a deal killer. It depends on which type of partnership you buy into.

General Partnership

A general partnership is, for all intents and purposes, a partnership where all the partners share everything. Now, as mentioned above, this is pretty straightforward when it comes to profit distribution. It is also very easy to see how initial capital requirements are distributed among the partners. However, they share everything, as in everything. This also means legal liability.

Now, why is this a deal killer for a lot of people? Well, when you are in a general partnership, there is no difference between your personal assets and the assets of the company as far as legal liability is concerned. Put simply, if the general partnership you form ran into some sort of legal trouble, for example, you are a partner in a trucking company, and one of the trucks runs over somebody and that person sues. If the general partnership does not have enough money in its bank account to pay for the judgment, by law the claimant can go after the assets of all the general partners. This is a serious problem because you invested to grow your money. You did not invest to lose money. Investing in a general partnership, however, exposes you to that tremendous amount of legal liability.

The big advantage of general partnership, however, is if you want to play an active role in the company, you get that role. As a general partner, you can play a starring role in the companies you invest assuming that you are willing to put in the work, and you have the time. Generally speaking, people who have the risk tolerance to invest in general partnerships to begin with often invest in many different partnerships. They are truly in it for the distribution; they are not really in it to take an active hand. However, if you would like to take an active hand, a general partnership is structured in such a way that it can help you do that; however, it comes at a steep price. The legal exposure involved is usually a deal killer for many potential investors.

Limited Partnerships

Considering the legal liability exposure the general partnership has, there were many laws passed in the United States and elsewhere hat enabled people to invest in partnerships without the matching legal exposure. This is where limited partnerships come in. There is potential legal liability here; however, the exposure turns primarily on how active you are in the company. For example, if you heard that a friend was starting a business, and it uses a partnership form, and you invest, your liability will not be as big if you are not an active partner.

In other words, you are not making active decisions to run the company. You are not involved in day-to-day operations. Your primary reason in investing in the company is to get a share of the profits. In such a case, limited partnerships can provide some measure of legal protection, but it is still not enough. The fact that there is still a possibility that claimants can go after the partners' assets curbs limited partnerships' appeal. They definitely have more takers than general partnership, but their appeal is still rather limited.

Limited Liability Partnerships or Limited Liability Companies

Whether you are dealing with an LLP or an LLC, the great thing about this business for is that you are legally on the hook just for the amount of money you invested in the company. Put simply, if the company runs into some sort of legal trouble, the claimant can only claim assets under the company. It cannot claim the assets of partners of that company.

The LLC form is also beneficial when tax time comes. Unlike a corporation that is double taxed, a limited liability company uses a "pass-through" taxation system meaning your income from LLC is put on your tax forms as other income and is taxed once. With a corporation, you are actually taxed twice. The corporation has to pay its own income tax and then once you get a dividend, you get taxed for that. Accordingly, the money that eventually makes it to your hands has been hit by the taxman twice.

Limited liability companies do not have this problem. They have a pass-through system. The big downside to limited liability partnerships and limited liability companies is the amount of people that can participate in the company. The number of participants or owners depends on which jurisdiction the LLP or LLC is based in.

The Pros and Cons of Investing in Business Partnerships

To recap, the great thing in investing in business partnerships is the fact that, for a variety reasons, company founders may not be ready to form a corporation. This is just the nature of the beast. May be they feel that they are not ready; perhaps they have had bad experiences in the past. Whatever the case may be, they would rather keep things personal; they would somewhat keep things on an immediate person-to-person level. Unfortunately, if you are looking to invest your money so you can grow it, you are letting go or overlooking a large amount of potentially lucrative business investment opportunities by leaving business partnerships of whatever form off the table.

Still, considering the legal liabilities involved, you really need to do your research. You also have to make sure that you invest through proper state-sanctioned mechanisms. Depending on the jurisdiction you are in, there may be "sunshine laws" that govern private investment in business partnerships.

Furthermore, a key downside in business partnerships also involves its main advantage. The principal advantage, of course, is that there is a person-to-person or hands-on type of involvement by the founders. There is definitely that personal feel. This can also be a downside because if you do not get along with your partner, and there is no official separation between management of the company and the owners of the company, this can lead to all sorts of personal friction. It is not uncommon for business partnerships to fall apart due to incompatible personalities. This is also true when investing partners have a tremendous amount of disagreement with the founders of the company regarding where to take the company. Whenever two people get together, there is always opportunity not to see eye to eye. This happens across the board. The problem is this kind of fairly common disagreement can lead to serious problems in a general partnership structure.

Moreover, there is the psychological element of the general partners feeling that they are doing all the work while the "silent" partners are just standing back collecting profits. There may be a sense that the disproportionate amount of the hard work, toil, risk-taking and creativity required to take the business to the next level is not being properly compensated because the non-active partners are merely sitting back. It may seem illogical; it may seem irrational; however, unfortunately, this is the emotional truth.

At some level or other, it is common for general partners who are actually running the company day to day may feel that they are taking all the risks, handling all the pressure; and all they get is a share that may not be enough or might even be smaller than the share of silent partners whose main contribution to the enterprise was their initial investment. You need to balance these when considering to invest in general partnerships. There may be quite a bit of drama there if you are not careful.

Finally, another key disadvantage of general partnerships that may get in the way of otherwise investors involves the issue of exit. Whenever you are investing in anything, make sure that there is some sort of exit mechanism. With stocks, entering and exiting a position is extremely easy. Just open an account, pick a stock, and set a limit order. Once the price dips to your limit order, the system automatically buys for you. You then set another limit order to sell at a certain point that matches your percentage profit target. If the stock hits that point soon the system executes it automatically, and you have exited the stock.

This is not the case with business partnerships. In many cases, you might have to advertise for somebody to take your place. Again, state law as well as federal law might get in the way because you cannot just advertise to the general public and expect people to buy. They do not know you from Adam. You also have to advertise to the right people and to the correct channels. This can sometimes cost you some cash.

Furthermore, there might not be an exit because if the partnership involves a fairly a small company, the risk might be too high for investors. Seriously, they do not know the founding partners like you do. They do not know them on a professional basis. They definitely do not know them on a personal basis. This limits your exit to a small population of people - people who know the founders. Still, there are quite lucrative opportunities in partnerships. You just have to have the patience, attention to detail and willingness to work your personal networks to sniff out these opportunities.

One key reason why partnerships may be the way for you to invent your money is that, in many cases, they require very little investments like less than a hundred thousand dollars, but in the hands of the right founders, that hundred thousand dollars can easily turn into millions of dollars. Believe it or not a lot of large companies that became corporations later started out as much smaller companies formed by partnerships.

Chapter 11: Investing in Private Corporations

As I mentioned in Chapter 10, some company founders do not jump in with both feet to form a corporation. In the beginning, they may have started a partnership. Many start on LLC, but generally speaking, people who start corporations right off the bat tend to look at other legal forms to start with. The reason should not be a surprise. As mentioned in the previous chapter, corporations are taxed twice. If you are a founding share holder and you work for the corporation, you get the dubious honor of being taxed three times. Sounds crazy, right? Well, let us step through it.

First, most jurisdictions view corporations as "persons" as far as the law is concerned. A corporation has rights. In the United States, a corporation has certain constitutional rights. Accordingly, just the government taxes individual persons, the government also taxes corporations. When a corporation turns a profit, that money is taxed. When that money is apportioned the distribution, called dividends, is also taxed. Finally, if you are a member of the corporation, and you work at the corporation; you get your income from the corporation; and your income is taxed. That is a lot of taxes. That is the reason why a lot of people are gun shy when it comes to investing in corporations.

The good news is that there are also a lot of reasons why corporations are more attractive than partnerships, especially general partnerships, as investments. Many entrepreneurs start private corporations as a way of avoiding personal legal liability should the corporation run into legal trouble. If a corporation is sued, the plaintiff is entitled only to the assets of the corporation unless the corporation was used as an alter ego of the people behind the corporation. Outside of that remote situation, legal liability pretty much begins and ends with the assets of the corporation.

This is why a lot of companies that take in investors are incorporated. Instead of buying a partnership, you buy shares in the company. Also, in terms of exit methods, you have a lot more available to you than if you were invested in a general partnership.

The Benefits of a Corporation

The biggest benefit of course has been mentioned already: limited legal liability. Outside of that, a corporation also has two serious benefits that make it much more attractive investment vehicle than partnerships. First, a corporation, technically speaking, can live forever. Seriously. If the company is making enough money year after year, it can get renewed and continue in operation. It can easily outlive the people who originally founded the corporation.

This is a big deal because if you invested in a general partnership, and one of the general partners dies, the partnership can readily dissolve. Also, there are all sorts of succession issues, and this can open a whole new can of worms. Not so with corporations. Succession is fairly straightforward. Lots of corporations have succession plans. Furthermore, if the company is making enough revenues, it can keep going for a long, long time.

Second, it is easier to dispose of your investment in the corporation by simply selling your shares. Unlike stocks that have a ready market and are extremely liquid, private corporations are a lot less liquid. Why? You have to be a sophisticated investor to buy into a private corporation that you did not found, or you are not related to. By "related to," I am referring to a situation where you are investing in a company that was not founded by your friends, relatives or any close associates. In other words, it is a total stranger who founded the company is selling shares to the public.

Such share offers are controlled and regulated by state and federal law. They require people buying into private corporations to be "sophisticated" investors. This is just a fancy legal term for people who can afford to lose money. Put simply you have so much cash, and you have made enough money through investing or founding businesses that you really will not lose out all that much if you invest in a bad company. There are certain net worth thresholds that you have to meet to be legally considered a sophisticated investor.

The other approach to investing in a private corporation is to be a founder. You can be named as the founder. As long as you know the people or you know people who know the people who founded the company, you can be listed as a founder. Accordingly, you do not have to jump through all the many legal hurdles put in an investor's way by the law.

Finally, you can buy private placements through certain private placement specialists. Now, this is where things can get a bit dicey. Private placement is basically like buying stock but for private corporations. The companies that facilitate these sales of shares have to comply with often stringent state and federal regulations. Generally speaking, novice investors are discouraged from buying private placements under of course, in the eyes of the law, they are sophisticated investors.

Quick Note on "S" Corporations

There is kind of a "hybrid" solution for corporate forms in the United States. You do not necessarily buy into a "full" corporation also known as a "C" corporation. Instead, you can buy into an "S" corporation. The great thing about the "S" corporation is that it is like an LCC but it has shares. In other words, it gives you pass through taxation and limited legal liability. The downside is an "S" corporation can only have a certain number of shareholders. If it goes past a particular threshold, its charter is violated.

The Advantages of Buying into Private Corporations

The big advantage of buying into a private corporation is that, first of all, you have legal protection as far as your personal liability exposure is concerned. Second, a lot of the companies that are offering private placements tend to be further along in their development stage. Of course, this does not apply across the board. There can certainly be corporations that just got founded and simply need shareholders; however, by and large, when founders use the private corporation format, they already have better sales; they have some kind of traction; and some sort of milestones have been reached. Again, this does not apply across the board, but generally speaking, when you buy into a corporation through a private placement, the company is a bit more developed.

Compare this with the general partnership situation where the partner has an idea; another partner puts in a few bucks; they work through the business for a few years. It is now panning out. They are struggling and then with a few more tweaks, and a little more money invested; they start turning things around, and after enough time has passed, they are making real money.

This is not the case with a private corporation giving up private placements. The fact that it has been able to give out private placements; it at least means it has enough resources to pay for the accountants and lawyers needed to make it through all the necessary regulations. Accordingly, you get some measure of confidence when buying into a private corporation. You can rest assured that it is not just some sort of fly-by-night company that was put together to try to rip people off. Do not get me wrong; that still happens but, by and large, by being required to go through the private placement process, there is some sort of filtering involved. At the very least, shady characters are scared off from offering shares this way because of all the regularity hurdles.

The Disadvantages of Buying into Corporations

The big disadvantage with buying into corporations depends on taxation. If you are buying into a type "C" corporation, you are going to get taxed twice. The corporate income is taxed, and then the dividends are taxed. The other disadvantage is a simple matter of discovery. Now, while there are private placement companies that try to get sophisticated investors interested in buying into private corporations, the company they are pushing might be a bit more developed; however, this does not necessarily mean that the company is worth investing in. Sure, a company might be established, but it does not mean that it is going to be profitable.

A company might be well regulated and properly set up; however, it does not necessarily mean that the people running the enterprise have the vision and genius needed to turn the enterprise into a success. Accordingly, finding good corporations to buy into really turns on the amount of time and attention to detail you have. Moreover, even if you were given a lot of offers to get into private corporations, this does not necessarily mean that you have to go ahead and invest. It may well turn out that there are no good companies there that can give you the return you are looking. Now, this does not mean that they are going to go belly up tomorrow. This does not mean that they are all badly run.

What this does mean is as an investor, you are looking for a certain return and the fact that you are investing in a private corporation instead of a public corporation means you are taking a lot more risks. Accordingly, you want to be properly compensated for the risks you are taking. So, the target ROI that you should have is probably going to be a little higher because this is more speculative. Keeping all these factors in mind, finding good corporations that are lucrative enough to invest in will definitely take quite a bit of work. It is not impossible but you really need to hustle a bit harder.

Chapter 12: Investing in Precious Metals

What if the government of the United States faced an internal and external threat and imploded? I know it sounds crazy; I know that it is almost impossible; nevertheless, humor me for a second. If everything were to disappear tomorrow, what do you think the value of your stocks would be? What do you think the value of your home would be? Do you think you could show up to work to earn a wage tomorrow? Do you think you can collect your rent from your tenant tomorrow?

Ask these questions because these are the kinds of "end times" or "apocalyptic" scenarios that few people entertain. However, if you look at the whole of human history, empires come and go. Governments come and go. Countries come and go. You really cannot take anything for granted. You truly cannot assume that a lot of the political and economic structures that you have gotten used to will continue forever. You simply need to look at a typical country in Africa or South America and in many places in Asia, and you can quickly see how temporary fortunes can be.

I raise the issue of impending collapse because during such times, there is really only one type of asset that you can count on to have value when everything hits the fan. I am of course talking about gold, silver, platinum and other precious metals. Whenever there is a tremendous amount of political upheaval, you can bet on precious metals to tide you through.

For example, during the fall of China to the communists in 1949, a columnist noticed that one of the generals had to be carried by a dozen men on board a plane. He was asking himself why this general had to be carried. He did not need a wheelchair; the person looked relatively healthy. Why did all these huge strapping dudes have to hoist the general up to the plane to make sure that he gets on it? Well, it turns out that the general was wearing a special suit that was lined with thick plates of gold. Put simply, he knew that the end of the old order was near, and the only thing that he could trust at the time was gold.

Sure enough, whenever there are times of political and economic chaos, the price of gold in the area experiencing those troubles spikes up. This is when people with assets would convert all their other assets like cash and stocks and bonds into gold. That is how important gold is. While there are many industrial precious metals out there, if you are looking for the classic standard of value, you do not have to look further than gold.

Gold has always been synonymous with wealth. In all four corners of the world, gold is valuable. Sure, currently stocks are more profitable, and people who invest in gold tend to settle for returns that underperform the market, but when everything crashes, you can bet that gold will not only retain its value, but its value will actually spike up. Gold has always spiked up.

Why Buy Gold?

Precious metal assets encompass more than gold. You can buy silver. You can buy platinum. You can buy other heavy industrial metals that are valued like gold. They will always have value. However, if you are looking for the quintessential precious metal to invest in, you need to look no further than gold or maybe silver.

Why buy gold? First of all, gold is easy to buy. Whether you are buying in Dubai, Middle East or Southeast Asia or in the Americas or Africa, gold is standardized as long as you are not buying jewellery, and you are just buying plain gold metal, gold is pretty much fungible. Fungible is a fancy term for saying interchangeable. In other words, when you get your gold bullion or gold unit tested in Argentina, the chemical results for that analysis would be the same if you got it tested in Japan or Africa or the Philippines.

Accordingly, it is easy to buy because it is highly standardized, and the price is widely known. You only need to go online and look up the current real-time market price of gold, and there you have the price of the gold item you are holding in your hand. Not only is it easy to buy, it is also easy to sell for the same reasons. There is no guess work involved. There is no need to authenticate the artwork of your gold bar because you are just selling and buying the plain metal. Now, if you were selling gold jewellery, then that is another matter entirely because there is a craftsmanship involved.

Another key reason why gold is a good investment is the fact it has always been associated with "real wealth." Next to land and real estate, when people are asked to define riches or wealth, they often think in terms of gold. They do not think in terms of paper money. Historically, people do not think of paper money. Paper money can come and go.

For example, when you look at the history of South America for the past 100 years, you would notice that economies crash and burn and rise up all the time. When it does this, there is some massive inflation. A lot of the cash that has been circulating is vaporized in value. Now, if people were trading in gold, the value would remain the same. In fact, the value would go up because of the economic uncertainty in that particular area. This is why people define "real wealth" in terms of gold. They know that it is genuine. It is worth something.

Partly driving the value of gold is its industrial uses. It has a tremendous amount of use in electronics, and also in heavy industry. At the very least, there will be some sort of market demand for gold even if people stop looking at it as something pretty enough to wear. There is still that base industrial demand for gold parts and gold plating. Similarly, gold has value because of its use as jewellery. This also drives up the global demand for, and by extension, its price. People have been setting diamonds and precious stones in gold settings, rings, earrings, necklaces and what have you.

Another great reason to buy gold is that in the off-chance governments and economies crash, your asset's value will be maintained. In other words, it routines its value. Now, keep in mind that the United States has a very stable economy and government. It is not going to go away any time soon. However, the United States also depends on other countries. It does not exist in a vacuum. If those other countries start to give way or if there is some sort of international turbulence, or there is some massive global banking or financial crash, you can bet that not only would your precious metal assets retain their value, but their value might even go up.

Finally, a key reason why it is a good idea to invest in precious metals like gold is the concept of inflation. Every single year, the dollars you have saved in the bank as well as stored in your wallet go down. It buys less and less goods and services with each passing year. Now, on a year-to-year basis, you might not feel much of a change. However, if you look at the timeline long enough, and if there is enough economic disturbances and turbulence, inflation can actually spike up.

This happened in the United States with food inflation. When it comes to certain food items like beef, commodity prices have actually doubled. Inflation is more pronounced in some other countries. For example, in the Philippines and India, inflation is so heavy that you only need to look back a few dozen years to realize how much you could have bought with one peso or with one Indian rupee. That is inflation for you, and there is no way of stopping it. It will always keep going because countries' currencies are no longer tied to the value of gold.

In the present global economic order, money only has value because the government says it has value. This is called "fiat" currency, and as you can tell, this all depends on trust. When people trust the government to keep its act together, then the money has value. When people do not trust the government or the government has embarked on really dangerous economic policies, the value of the currency tanks.

A recent example of this is when Zimbabwe, which used to be the bread basket of Southern Africa, underwent a massive land reform. This caused such economic turbulence that there was little trust in the currency. The government was actually printing out currency that had a face value of trillions, and it was still not enough to buy something as basic as a loaf of bread. Put simply, trust in the government can only go so far, and that is why there is inflation. Some places have higher inflation; other places have lower inflation, but inflation still exists.

The only country in recent memory that does not suffer from inflation is Japan. People had such tremendous respect for the Japanese government that people were actually hoarding their yen. They are net savers, not spenders.

You might think that this is a great thing, but deflation is definitely what is causing a lot of Japan's economic woes. Decreasing prices is just as harmful as rising prices. When people feel that the price of something would be lower next year than the current year, then they would hold back. They would wait for the prices to get even lower. Well, the problem is the factories need to employ people now.

When people do not buy because of prices are drooping, companies hire less and less people. This starts a chain reaction that ultimately is bad for the economy. Regardless of how you feel about inflation; it is a fact of life. In one of the best hedges against inflation is gold. Gold has its own intrinsic value. The great thing about gold is when inflation jacks up the prices of everything like rent, food, utilities; the price of gold goes up. Inflation does not decrease its spending power.

The Disadvantages of Precious Metals

Well, there is no such thing as a perfect investment. Investing in precious metals will not make all your investment woes go away. First of all, if you invest in physical gold, it can get really bulky. You better have a large safe, and you better put the safe in the basement or in the bottom floor o6f your home. You would not want your roof to cave in because gold is very heavy.

Now, the good news is that you do not have to store physical gold. You can invest in exchange-traded funds or ETFs that buy gold as a physical metal. This is as close as you can get to speculating on the real-time value of gold.

The bigger disadvantage in investing in gold is the fact that in recent years, gold's investment performance has trailed stocks and bonds. During serious growth eras of stock markets, gold is often a laggard. There have been many financial advisers who have been telling people to load up on gold for several years. Sadly, their clients who took up their advice end up underperforming the market.

Now, this does not mean that they are out of money. This does not mean that inflation killed the value of their investment. This does not mean that. What this means is that if the stock market appreciated 15% year after year, these gold investors may have been stuck with a 10% annual appreciation. In other words, they could have made more money if they invested in other asset classes.

Considering how powerful gold's value has been historically, a lot of people are claiming that the modern economy is just set up in such a way that gold is no longer the fool-proof investment it used to be. I would not go that far. A lot of the global stock market's performance has been fuelled by government fiscal policy rather than solid economic performance.

Take the case of the US Federal Reserve. Right after the financial crash, the Federal Reserve undertook the fiscal policy of buying up debt. This stabilized the market, but this was also completely artificial. The reason why this was "successful" was because of the huge trust the global investing community had in the United States. If this was undertaken by another government with less than stellar global trust, the results may not have been all that positive.

Put simply, quantitative easing just highlighted the fact that the global financial system no longer runs on classic economic fundamentals of value. Instead, it all runs on government fiat and trust. Keep this in mind when considering gold. Do not think that just because gold has been underperforming stocks in the past years that this would be a trend that would persist forever. After all, gold has been around for thousands and thousands of years while the US dollar is still less than 300 years old.

Gold Variation

Another way you can invest in precious metals without buying ETFs or buying gold bullion or gold plates is to purchase jewellery. If you are into jewellery, this is a great way of buying precious metals. Consider it a wearable asset. The downside to buying gold or precious metals this way is that you actually pay more than the base value of the metal. This is not rocket science because to create a piece of jewellery, a craftsman has to work the metal.

Keep this in mind. When you buy jewellery as an investment, the premium you pay for the craftsmanship may be too high. Furthermore, the jewellery might not appreciate value against inflation. This is not always the case. There are certain jewellery lines and jewellery "brands" that actually command a premium over the base metal value of the gold the jewellery pieces contain.

Chapter 13: Investment Vehicles

Now that we have covered the many different ways you can invest and the many different asset classes you can invest in, as well as the importance of risk profile and risk appetite, the next step is to focus on how you're going to invest.

A lot of Americans think that there is only one way to invest in stocks. A lot of people are under the impression that they only need to buy mutual funds and they're good to go. While there is a lot recommending mutual funds, and I've gone into some length in outlining their advantages, a lot of people feel that mutual funds are too constricting.

Make no mistake about it, if you are going to buy individual stocks and you pick the right stocks, you are going to outperform mutual funds all day, every day. Seriously. Even if you have a moderate risk profile, direct investment in the right stocks will blow away mutual funds' performance every single year.

Now, the big problem here should be obvious: most people don't know what the "right" stocks are. People were clueless yesterday, people are clueless now, and people will continue to be clueless in the future. It's anybody's guess. That's why mutual funds remain popular. If you were to try to do your own individual stock risk diversification program, depending on how you put it together, you might just be better off investing in stocks through mutual funds.

The good news is, the US Tax Code allows for different investment vehicles that may have tremendous tax advantages. This can free up your hand as you experiment with which investment strategy to take. While it's always a good idea to devote a certain percentage of your total investment portfolio in mutual funds, you might also want to play around with individual stock buys or individual asset buys.

In this chapter, I'm going to step you through two investment vehicles that are provided for by the US Tax Code. According to the US Tax Code, individuals can put away a certain amount of money every year which will be shielded from taxes. This is called the individual retirement account or IRA or 401K Programs.

You might be thinking that these are one and the same. No, they're not. There is a big difference between a 401K and an IRA. An IRA is an account you set up for yourself. In fact, it's self explanatory, in the name of the account. It is, after all, called an individual retirement account. This account goes with you wherever you go. Whether you work at one job and quit that and move on to another job, you will always have that IRA that you can fund.

A 401K, on the other hand, is a retirement fund that has a matching component from your employer. Whatever amount of money you put into the 401K, your employer will match, up to a certain cap.

Ideally, most people should invest in both vehicles. They should have a 401K at work and an individual retirement account. However, given the economic realities of most American households, this is too much to ask for. In fact, generally speaking, Americans just have a 401K, assuming they even have that at all.

Regardless of what investment vehicle you have, please pay attention to the following discussion because it will step you through the things you can do with these investment vehicles. You'd be surprised as to the kind of assets you can put into an IRA, for example.

401Ks

401Ks are stipulated by law to encourage Americans to set aside money for their retirement. The big incentive with 401Ks is that their employers can match the amount that they put in. This pushes individuals to put away a certain amount from each paycheck into their 401K account. Of course, there is an absolute cap on how much money can be put into this account by the employer as well as the employee.

There are also certain tax advantages that flow from a 401K account. It's not like a typical stock trading account where you are taxed per transaction.

The big advantage of a 401K is that you have a built-in psychological incentive to invest. Think of it as free money. For every dollar you put in, your employer is going to match that dollar. There is a tremendous psychological boost inherent in that "free dollar" that you are getting, courtesy of your employer.

The big disadvantage of 401Ks is that you have to roll them over when you move from employer to employer. This is a big deal if you are in an industry where people tend to move around a lot. Also, this can be an issue when you stop working for an employer and you start working for yourself. Also, depending on the type of 401K set up, there might be serious restrictions on the type of assets you can invest in.

Individual Retirement Accounts - Two Flavors

Believe it or not, there are actually two flavors of individual retirement accounts. There is the regular IRA that you can set up for yourself and fund voluntarily through the rest of your life and use it as an investment vehicle for stocks, bonds and REITs and other asset classes. With the regular IRA, you're taxed per transaction. When you sell stocks and you made a profit, you are taxed right after the sale.

The other flavor of IRA is the Roth IRA. The great thing about this investment vehicle is that it performs just like a regular IRA, but with one key difference. You're only taxed when you redeem your IRA. In other words, only when you start taking out money from your IRA will you get taxed.

This tax deferral is a big boon because if you think about it, this tax deferment acts as a compounding mechanism that enables you to take what you could have spent on taxes and use it to buy more asset and then grow your asset base until you're ready to retire. Up at that point, once you start making withdrawals from your account, you then start paying taxes.

Depending on how your investments do and how you play your cards, this can mean a huge difference in terms of asset appreciation. For every dollar you invest in your Roth IRA, as opposed to a regular IRA, your buck might actually go much further.

Another great thing about IRA that newbie investors should pay attention to is its flexibility. A regular IRA or a Roth IRA can actually accommodate a broad range of asset classes. You can invest in precious metals, for example. You don't even have to invest in ETFs necessarily. You can invest in other forms of gold or precious metal securities like the stocks of gold mining companies. These mining stocks don't necessarily have to be in the NASDAQ or NYSE. They can also be pink sheets, bulletin board and even emerging market stocks.

The flexibility of IRAs enable you to take better risks. By better risks, I'm not talking about necessarily mitigating your risks or reducing your risk level. Instead, I'm talking about increasing your risk in an educated way so you could increase the return that you get.

As I have kept repeating in this book, the higher the risk, the higher the reward. You just have to make sure that you are taking educated risks. Junk bonds, for example, issued by fast growing companies that either dominate or are close to dominating their industries are educated risks. You get a nice yield compared to "safer" investments.

Chapter 14: Getting Organized: How to Form Your Own Personal Investing Plan

It is my hopes that after you've read through the 13 chapters of this book that you're excited about investing. Believe me, the worst thing that you can do to your hard earned dollars is to put it in a bank. For every month your money is stuck in a bank, it is going down in value. Welcome to the world of inflation.

Sure, we live in fairly unusual times where inflation is at a historic low. Thanks to Alan Greenspan and his successors, the interest rate climate in the United States has changed dramatically. Historically, interest rates in the US have hovered over 5%. In other countries, particularly developing countries, you'd be lucky to have an interest rate climate that is between 4-7% year after year.

Inflation, for lack of a better phrase, is an asset killer. Every year you keep your assets in the form of cash, the value of your assets goes down. This is why it's crucial to start looking at ways to invest your money to turn $1 into $2 or more.

It's not going to happen overnight. There are many different options out there, and I have outlined them in this book, but what's important is that you decide to start an investing plan today.

Here are just some tips on how to get on the road to a personal investing plan that can produce a tremendous amount of assets in the future. Keep in mind that the sooner you start, the better your returns would be. Thanks to compounding, a difference of as little as 5-10 years can translate to a huge amount of dollars when it comes time for you to retire.

Start as soon as possible if you can. It doesn't have to be a lot of money. As long as you resolve to start small and then scale up your contributions, you will be fine. Also, if you are young, and I'm talking about people who are below the age of 30, you can invest in riskier asset classes, which can have a tremendous effect on the total rate of appreciation of your investment portfolio.

Automatic Deductions

The first thing that you should do if you are employed is to apply for an automatic deduction program with your employer. Ask that a certain percentage of your income be deducted automatically from your paycheck, straight to either an IRA, a Roth IRA or your employer's 401K program.

If you don't work for other people or you're self-employed or you own your own business, then you need to come up with a monthly or a quarterly schedule for investment set asides. You essentially look at your earnings for the quarter and start piling up cash to be invested every 3 months or every 4 months.

Automatic Investment Schedule

Now that you have money set aside, keep in mind that it doesn't matter how little capital you have to work with. The amount doesn't matter as much as the fact that you have actually decided to start investing. Congratulate yourself if you decided to follow through and start investing.

The next step is to set up a schedule for your investments. This is very important because what you need to do is to look at your risk profile and make percentage distributions depending on your profile. For example, if you are under the age of 30, a large chunk of your investment portfolio should be in stocks. Among those stocks, you can get away with devoting a large percentage of your investment to internet stocks, new media stocks and other fast rising sectors.

On the other hand, if you're older, for example, you're over the age of 50, a large chunk of your investments should be in more conservative asset classes like tax-free municipal bonds, Triple A rated and very safe corporate bonds and similar investments. You should also consider commercial rental real estate for recurring passive income.

Set up an automatic investment schedule by figuring out the asset classes you're going to invest in and the type of risks involved and start making asset purchases. Again, this has to take place on a schedule. You can't just make purchases when you feel like it or when you have time.

This has to be automatic, otherwise, it's too easy to give yourself all sorts of excuses as to why you can't get around to investing this month or this quarter. Soon enough, it will turn into a habit and you would have failed to invest much of anything.

Pool "Free" Investment Cash for Maximum Flexibility

While it's important to stick to a schedule, it's also important to make sure that you have a certain percentage devoted to cash. Now, you're not hanging on to cash for the sake of hanging on to cash. As I've already mentioned several times, inflation is going to destroy your assets. Instead, you keep a certain percentage in cash to enable you to quickly take advantage of investment opportunities as they materialize.

For example, you may have heard of a commercial property that is usually worth several hundred thousand dollars, but is being liquidated in a fire sale. You may come across a situation where an awesome stock that has a tremendous potential and has passed positive performance hit a rough patch and crashed really hard. It may be a good idea to pounce on that stock at that time. Regardless of the form the opportunity takes, it's always a good idea to have enough free cash available so you can take advantage of such opportunities as they materialize.

Steady and Consistent Wins Over Time

Now, here comes the rough part. It's easy to think that once you invest in "the right stock," you will become a millionaire overnight. While it is true that some investors hit it big, this is not a practical strategy. It's much better to focus on a steady and consistent investing strategy instead of simply picking the "one right stock" or "one right investment" and making it big overnight.

While it does happen from time to time, chances are, in your situation, it won't. It's a much better use of your time and resources to focus on a steady and consistent investment plan using diversified assets instead of just simply picking out one stock that would turn you into a millionaire seemingly overnight.

Chapter 15: Investment Strategies

Now that you have a clear idea of why you need to invest and some very important principles in investment as well as asset classes you can invest in, the next step is to come up with a winning investment strategy.

Now you probably have come across many different basic investing books that claim to have some sort of "golden strategy" that would enable you to win every single time. While that is entirely possible, getting to that point takes quite a bit of work.

In other words, for you to start winning in a big way, you would have to put in the time. You would have to put in the effort. You would have to have the proper experience and groundwork to make that happen. And in many cases, even with the best laid plans and even with the best strategies laid out, things still don't pan out.

The better approach is to do the best with the situation you are facing. In other words, use certain strategies that would enable you to position yourself to come out ahead. They might not necessarily result in you making tons of money or experiencing truly stupendous returns, but they can position you for solid gains. The following strategies enable you to do just that.

Buy Depressed Assets

Now, this might seem pretty straightforward. After all, this is really just a reiteration of the classic investment and commercial maxim of "buy low, sell high." No big mystery there. However, the big challenge here is in determining what constitutes a "depressed asset."

You might be thinking that a stock that was trading at $50 and pop to $150 might not be all that depressed if it fell to $100. You might be thinking, where's the depression? This is not a fire sale. It hasn't fallen enough.

Well, if you look at the trajectory of the stock and how much growth potential there is as well as market attention, it might very well turn out that the stock is headed to $300. Do you see how this works?

If that's the case, then scooping up the stock at the price of $100 after it fell from $150 is a steal. After all, buying something that is worth $300 for a third of its price is one heck of a bargain. It doesn't take a rocket scientist to figure that out.

Now, the big issue here, of course, is how do you know the stock's full future value? This is where serious analysis comes in. You can't just buy stocks on a hunch. You can't just buy stocks on hype. You need to look at facts that would inform the growth trajectory of that stock.

For example, is it a market leader? Does it have certain drugs in the approval pipeline that have little to no competition? Is it on the cusp of a breakthrough drug patent? Is it in the process of buying out its competition?

There are many factors that you should consider which can impact the overall future value of a stock. You should pay attention to its current developments and you should pay attention to the news cycle surrounding the company.

You should also pay attention to its industry. Is its industry fast expanding or is it a "sunset industry" that is on its last legs? If it's in a sunset industry, there might still be opportunities there because usually, such industries witness a tremendous amount of consolidation. Whatever the case may be, always be on the lookout for the future value of a stock based on what you know now, as well as its past performance.

Dollar Cost Averaging

What happens if you buy a stock that subsequently crashes? Believe me, this happens to the very best of us. If this happened to you, don't get depressed. Don't think that you suck at investing. Don't think that all is lost. In fact, if you get caught in a downturn, it might actually be an amazing opportunity.

Now, it's important to note that almost all stocks experience a pullback. I have yet to come across a stock that has appreciated positively with no dips in its whole trading history. I'm not aware of a stock that hasn't experienced at least a day to day dip in pricing. All stocks experience a pullback. Even stocks that are well on their way to becoming breakthrough or high-valued stocks will experience dips.

I need to get that out of the way because it's easy to think that you made a foolish bet buying at the "very top." Well, that "very top" might actually just be the beginning of a peak that is soon to be replaced by another peak after the stock hit a valley. Keep that in mind.

So what do you do if you get caught in a downturn? What happens if you bought a stock that drops in value tremendously? Well, you have 2 options at this point in time. You can wait for the stock to keep going up and then start buying some more. You're basically taking bets on its recovery.

The better approach would be to use this as an opportunity. For example, if you bought, for the sake of simplicity, one share of stock at $100 a share, and the price crashes 50% to $50 a share, you can buy one share at $50 and this would average out your holdings to $75 per share.

Ideally, you should wait for the stock to drop so much and then buy a whole lot. This enables you to set your break-even point at a much lower level. For example, using the same hypothetical facts mentioned above, instead of buying one share, you buy 9 shares at $50. So what happens is, the average price per share gets reduced to $55.

In other words, even if the depressed stock just manages to limp along and possibly pop up here and there, it doesn't have to pop up all that much for you to get all your money back from your position because once it hits $55, you're at break even territory. Compare this with breaking even at $75 or, worse yet, waiting for the stock to come back to $100 a share. It's anybody's guess whether it will back to that level.

This strategy is called dollar cost averaging and it is very, very effective. However, for this to work, you have to take my advice in the previous chapter of pooling "free investment cash." You have to have free cash available and, most importantly, you have to use that free cash at the right time.

That's how you maximize its value. That's how you fully take advantage of opportunities that present themselves. Otherwise, you might be in a situation where the stock crashes so hard that you could have broken even very easily with little money spent, but unfortunately, you were locked out because you don't have the cash to do it.

The good news is, if you are using an online broker that has decent margin facilities, you can borrow the money that you use to buy the stock at the depressed price from your margin account. Now, there's a big danger here. This is not a slam dunk by any means.

You have to make sure that you are investing in stocks that have a high likelihood of recovering because if the stock goes further south and the price drops even more, you are in a worse position. Not only are you not averaging your costs, but you are also going to be under pressure to pay back your broker. In fact, they can and do liquidate positions to cover the amount you owe.

Use this facility, as powerful as it is, only if you are very confident that the stock will recover somewhat. Trading on margin in usually a good idea if you're doing dollar cost averaging after the stock has crashed tremendously, as in it gets really close to zero.

Buy Self Liquidating Assets

Another investing strategy you can take is to buy assets that pay for themselves. For example, if you spent a million dollars buying a building, but the building generates rents totaling $100,000 per year, the building pays for itself in roughly 13 years or more, factoring taxes and other costs.

Self liquidating assets may seem too good to be true, but they are very real. Most of this applies to certain types of real estate like commercial properties. However, this strategy also applies to stocks and bonds.

For example, if you buy stocks that have no dividend and you buy bonds, you can use the bond interest to start paying off your stocks portfolio. Of course, this can take quite a bit of time if you factor in interest rates as well as taxes.

Smart Money Valuation

Another winning strategy is to buy into private corporations as a sophisticated investor at a much lower valuation. Now keep in mind that there are many mobile app companies popping up all over the place in the United States. You don't necessarily have to live in Silicon Valley of California to have access to these types of companies.

The great thing about these companies is that in the beginning, they require very little capital. In fact, many require "Angel," "per-Angel" or even raw seed capital. Basically, the founder would just have a rough idea of a software, an app or a website. This is the most basic stage of a company's evolution.

Now, when you come in as a source of seed capital, you can actually lock into a large chunk of the stock of the company for a very low valuation. For example, somebody comes up with a startup idea and the initial valuation of the company is maximum $1 million. If you were to come in and invest $250,000, you have a 25% stake in the company.

Now, you may be thinking, 25% of a company that's not really worth that much, which is very, very risky, doesn't seem like a winning proposition. Well, keep in mind that after the seed stage, the valuation of the company usually goes up. So once your money has been used to push the company further along in its developmental path, the company's valuation starts to go up, especially if they now have something more concrete to show other investors.

When they start showing the software prototype, the mobile app or the website or whatever it is that the company's building to angel investors, the valuation is usually much higher. At that point, it's not uncommon for a company that has a seed valuation of $100,000 or $500,000 to look like a company that is worth $1 million or more. In other words, the valuation of your initial investment just doubled. And the best part is that you only put in money and let the founders do their thing.

Once their company gets past the angel stage and the product that was funded starts generating money and the company looks like it's on firmer foundation, it's anybody's guess what the succeeding valuations would be. A company can very well go from a valuation of $150,000 to $500,000 when you came in, to $1 million at the angel round, and to $5 million once the company starts generating revenues.

You see, your investment doesn't exist in a vacuum. You're actually funding the operations of an enterprise that is doing something with the money. It's not like the money is just being sucked up by the founders and being used for personal purposes. If you invest in a company that is professionally run, that money is going directly towards the development of the underlying product or service that the company offers.

Once the company starts generating revenue, you can pretty much sit pretty because even though your percentage will be diluted as the company's number of shares expand, the value of the money you invested at least is locked in. For example, if you've invested $100,000 in a company that had an initial valuation of $300,000, you have 33% ownership. You then get diluted when it goes to the angel stage and the company is now worth $3 million and your shares get further diluted as the valuation increases.

The good news here is that you don't have to necessarily wait for the company to issue shares through an initial public offering. You can ask subsequent investors to buy you out. This is a big deal because they're not going to buy you out based on the valuation that was used when you entered the company. Using the example above, you're not going to get bought out at the initial valuation of $300,000.

If the company, for example, is now valued at $15 million, that's what you're going to be bought out at and, believe me, you may have only invested $100,000, but your shares in the company will be worth a lot more than $100,000, considering the fact that you bought a fairly large chunk of the company for essentially a song.

Alternatively, you can just hang on to your shares and wait for the founders to either get the company bought out by an established company like Disney or Amazon, or, this is a moon shot, wait until the company goes IPO. Now, if the company has an initial public offering, and provided the stock doesn't tank permanently quickly after it goes public, this is your big payout because you essentially paid very, very little money for a significant percentage of a company that can possibly be worth several hundred million dollars, or even several billion dollars.

Now, you may be thinking that you only own 1% of the company after you got diluted, but considering the fact that you only paid $100,000 using the details of the example described above, that is very little money considering the fact that the company is worth hundreds of millions of dollars, if not billions of dollars.

For the sake of simplicity, let's say that you bought in at $100,000 and after the IPO, your total ownership of the stock is 1%, if the company is valued by the market at a conservative $250 million, you turned your $100,000 into $2 million. Not too shabby, right?

Finding Smart Money Valuation Opportunities

Now, you may be asking yourself, okay, the smart money valuation thing sounds awesome. This is great in theory, but is it real? How can the Average Joe investor get in on such deals?

Well, actually, there are websites like Angel List and others, as well as groups on LinkedIn that publicize startup projects that are actively recruiting investors. Of course, you need to do your homework.

Also, pay attention to the track record of the founders. Don't fall into the trap of investing in a "startup" that is founded by serial scammers. You probably would have to filter through a lot of ore to find a few gold nuggets.

The good news is, the gold nuggets do exist. You just have to do your homework. You just have to put in the time.

Conclusion

You bought this book because you are completely in the dark regarding investing. Congratulations, you have everything you need to know to start putting together a more formal investing plan.

You still need to do more research. You still need to ask yourself a lot of questions regarding your risk profile, your risk appetite and the types of asset classes you want to invest in. However, a lot of the initial heavy work has been taken care of. You have everything you need to know to start yourself on your way to greater and greater investing success.

I can't emphasize this enough: you have to start early when it comes to investing. The sooner you start, the easier you could recover from any missteps you may take in the future. You also stand to earn a lot more off your assets due to compound interest as well as overall asset value appreciation.

I hope you take all the information outlined in this book to heart, and I wish you the greatest investing success.

Finally, if you enjoyed this book and received value out of it then I'd like to ask you for a favor. Would you be kind enough to leave a review for this book on Amazon? It'd be greatly appreciated!

Leaving review only takes a few seconds and it will enable me to continue to produce high quality, enriching content to serve people like you.

As we learnt the powerful investing strategies, I want to reach as many people as I can with this book in order to share the benefits of these strategies to maximum people. The higher the number of reviews, the more people I can reach!

The more positive reviews the book gets, the more others will be able to find the book, purchase it and experience the benefits of investing.

Preview of

Stock Market Investing
For Beginners

Simple Stock Investing Guide To Become An Intelligent Investor And Make Money In Stocks

By David Morales

Available on Amazon

https://www.amazon.com/dp/1544770812

https://www.amazon.co.uk/dp/1544770812

Introduction

This is my personal stock trading story: I started trading stocks when I got my first part time job while I was still in college. You might think that this was a pretty great start. After all, most people never really start stock investing until they are already established in their careers. In fact, the average American trades stock primarily as a passive investor as part of that person's 401k plan at work. Put simply, most people don't actively look to invest in stocks.

You might think that I had a great early start with investing. Well, not quite. While Microsoft, Apple, Cisco and other amazing companies were trading at the time I started investing in stocks, I didn't invest in those stocks. If I did, I'd be worth hundreds of millions of dollars today. In fact, when I started investing, Cisco, Apple and Microsoft were trading at very low prices.

What I did was I just dove into stock investing and bought whatever "cheap" companies were being recommended by investment "experts" featured in the newspapers I read at that time. I only paid attention to two factors: the price of the stock and where it was in its 52 week valuation. If the stock was trading near its 52 week low, and the stock was affordable as far as my budget was concerned, I bought the stock.

I did not look into its industry, I did not do research regarding the company's market position. In many cases, I didn't even know if the company was making any money. I only looked at whether it was recommended by experts and whether it was cheap enough. Every pay check I would set aside a few hundred dollars to buy these "cheap" stocks I was told had a "tremendous upside."

As I mentioned, I didn't bother to do thorough industry research, nor did I pay attention to the stock's momentum, volume and other crucial trading details. The result? Of the 5 companies I invested in, 2 went bankrupt. One is still around, but it's a dormant "shell" company that is a penny stock. To make matters worse, it barely trades. The other two companies that I bought, I ended up selling them for prices that were lower than I bought them for.

Fast Forward to Today

Now, I make money on all my trades. I know when to buy in, and I know when to sell. In fact, it has become quite predictable to me. While I don't always rack up daily profits in the 5 digit range, I definitely have come a very long way from when I began trading. I actually make a profit every single day.

I've got some great news for you: if I can go from a hype-crazed foolish investor throwing good money after bad on lousy stocks to someone who can reliably pick winning stocks, so can you. The only difference between you and me is information.

This book spells out the information you need to begin your stock trading career the right way. Don't begin it the same way I did. I lost money. I worked hard for that money while I was going to college and all that money just went up in smoke. Learn from my mistakes.

Indeed, this book is a compilation of the hard lessons I've learned trading stocks through the years. Put simply, I focused on the things that work. I focused on the information you need to pay attention to so you can become a successful stock trader.

There are Tons of Investment Books Out There

Let's just get one thing out of the way, while it's true that this book is yet another of many stock investment books in the marketplace, most of those stock investment books have it all wrong. This book is intended to help newbie traders such as you to cut through the hype and fluff and get to the good stuff as quickly as possible.

You need to avoid my mistakes and benefit from what I got right. By getting the right information from the very beginning, you put yourself in a better position. You increase your chances of trading profitably, consistently. I can't emphasize the word "consistently" enough.

Make no mistake about it, anybody can get lucky from time to time. Unfortunately, luck is not going to put food on the table. Luck can fall short. You need a clear idea as to what works so you can trade with a higher chance of consistent profit.

Stock Trading is a Journey

I wish I could tell you that, just by reading this book, you will become a millionaire. Unfortunately, nobody can make that guarantee. You have to understand that stock trading is a journey. Just like any trip, it involves growth. It involves changing your perspective and, yes, it involves overcoming challenges.

This book steps you through the jungle of confusing "stock market talk" and terms and puzzling "strategies." Instead, I explain strategies in clear, everyday English, so you can make truly informed decisions when looking for trading opportunities, timing your buying and selling, and reinvesting your profits.

I wish you the very best in your journey into the amazing and richly rewarding world of stock trading!

---------------------------------End of Preview--------------------------------

CPSIA information can be obtained
at www.ICGtesting.com
Printed in the USA
BVHW082346160622
639979BV00004B/214